To
Dr. Mr. G. Brink
from
his old Teacher
John's Father

Binghamton
Jan 1 / 68.

Presented to
Annie Noakes.
By her friend
W. Brink.

F. S. Agate, pinxt.

S. H. Gimber, sculp.

JOHN D. LOCKWOOD.

# MEMOIR

OF

# JOHN D. LOCKWOOD.

BY REV. PETER LOCKWOOD

BINGHAMTON, N. Y.

SECOND EDITION REVISED BY THE AUTHOR.

PUBLISHED BY THE

AMERICAN TRACT SOCIETY,

150 NASSAU-STREET, NEW YORK.

# CONTENTS.

# MEMOIR

OF

# JOHN D. LOCKWOOD.

---

## CHAPTER I.

### FIRST SEVEN YEARS OF JOHN'S LIFE.

JOHN DAVENPORT LOCKWOOD was born Oct. 9, 1825, at the house of his maternal grandfather, Hon. John Davenport, Stamford, Conn.

From his infancy, he was considered as a remarkably interesting child—not only fair and prepossessing in his person, but amiable in his disposition, and giving indications that he possessed a mind of a high order. His mother has retained the following incidents:

"When between nine and ten months old, he showed a good deal of temper towards his father, which he thought necessary to correct. This was done by refusing to take him up from the floor, on which he was playing. The contest lasted for an hour, when he yielded, and came to his father with a subdued manner. After this his father never had to do more than speak, and he would yield immediately."

That scene in the parlor, I well remember. I considered it important not only to establish parental authority, but to settle in his mind the principle of filial submission and obedience. Though my heart was pained, and I many times wished that I had not begun the contest, yet the issue was actually joined, and I dared not yield. Knowing, moreover, that I was requiring nothing but what the child could perform, and the grandmother and other members of the family sustaining me by their countenance, I persevered till he came to me. All in a perspiration, he put up his face to mine, then laid his head upon my shoulder, and there soon fell asleep. I carried him to the nursery, and laid him on the bed, where he had a long nap. After which, according to previous arrangement, I went first to him and took him up.

Though the little creature had hardly ceased sobbing, he received me with a pleasant smile, and from that time to the day of his death, I cannot recall an instance in which he willingly disobeyed me; and never afterwards had I just occasion to punish him, or to find fault with him.

"He early showed," says his mother, "a great fondness for flowers; and when, being a year old, he was carried into a room where were a number of jars of flowers, he expressed his admiration by pointing his tiny finger, and exclaiming, O! O! as he was carried from one to another. This fondness increased with his years. It was always his delight to range the fields, and to gather flowers."

"His parents early discovered that he would be easily alarmed; and they endeavored to keep from him every thing of a frightful character. They never punished him by shutting him in a dark place.

"His father being absent a greater part of the time, for more than a year after he was nine or ten months old, his first religious instruction devolved upon his mother. Usually, instead of telling him how God punished the naughty and disobedient, she held HIM up as a God of love, and as grieved, or offended, if we disobeyed him. His first prayer was the little one by Dr. Watts, "Now I lay me down to sleep," etc. His next was a little form of prayer that God would bless his parents, his friends, himself, and make him a good boy; occasionally mentioning any particular fault he had been guilty of. He was very early taught the little child's catechism by Dr. Watts, and the commandments, as abbreviated. Being naturally very fond of stories, he was always delighted with scripture narratives, particularly with the story of Joseph and his brethren, as related by his father in simple language.

"His father was settled in Binghamton, N. Y., when he was two years old, but he was not taken to public worship on the Sabbath till six months after.

"Though very fond of handling books, he was not willing to learn his letters at first; and, at last, was not compelled to learn them. His parents, sensible that he was acquiring knowledge all the time, were not anxious that he should learn to read very early.

"When a little more than three years old, Miss Park, a young lady who had been accustomed to teach, came to reside in the family; and by her his parents feel that they were very much aided in governing and instructing their child.

"When about three and a half years of age, finding him willing to learn, she commenced teaching him his letters, which he learned in the course of two weeks. From that time he took an interest in learning to read. If at any time he showed an unwillingness to learn, he was stimulated to it by the motive of a desire for knowledge, and never for the sake of being superior to others.

"When four years old he could read the Bible. Before he was five, he went with his mother to visit his grandparents; when he was presented by his grandfather with a Bible, which he kept and read till it was worn out.

"He was not, at that age, permitted to have many associates; and those were three or four boys, a year or two older than himself.

"The winter after he was four, he fell down the garret stairs, and broke his leg. During the first two or three days, he suffered great pain. At such times, as he had always been told that in trouble we must pray to God, he would ask his father to pray with him—and prayer would always compose him.

"A little after this, his shoulder was dislocated by falling from a horse. Not long after, he received a severe gash in the calf of his leg, by a sharp, ragged piece of iron. Thus early was he called to endure pain. He could anticipate it with a good deal of resolution, and bear it with uncommon fortitude. Early in life, when suffering with the pain of an ulcerated tooth, he was sent alone to the doctor, to have it extracted. Meeting the doctor in the street, he hailed him, and delivering his message, climbed into the wagon, where the doctor, with his turnkey, drew out the offending member."

In the spring of 1829, the first serious effort was made to establish the cause of temperance in Binghamton. At that time two distilleries were in active operation in the village, in one of which an elder of the church was the distiller. Every merchant in the village kept ardent spirits for sale; and, as was then the case everywhere in our country, almost every family was in the habit of using it, or offering it to friends as a token of hospitality.

The discussion in that village was unusually warm. At length the cause of temperance triumphed. The elder relinquished his business in the distillery, although it was all his living. Both distilleries ceased operations. Nearly every merchant relinquished the traffic. And individuals and families were gradually abandoning the practice of using liquor themselves, or offering it as a beverage to their visitors.

In the course of this discussion, which continued several years, John took a decided stand in favor of temperance. And though of course he never mingled in debates, and was, as such a child should always be taught to be, only a listener and a spectator, especially when away from home, he was firmly resolved to have nothing to do with alcohol. And when, in the Sabbath-school, application was made for signatures to the pledge of total abstinence from ardent spirits, John sent in his name. A gentleman, then engaged in the traffic and manufacture of whiskey, an intimate friend of the family, on seeing John a few days afterwards, thus accosted him in a pleasant way: "John, they say *you* have joined the Temperance Society. What do you know about the Temperance Society? Say, John, do you know what you have done?" To this challenge, I am told, the child replied with great promptness, "Yes, I have promised not to drink any thing stronger than water as long as I live." At that time the pledge included only ardent spirits. John, however, always afterwards strictly kept the pledge as he understood it; abstaining not only from all vinous and fermented, as well as spirituous liquors, but also from tea and coffee.

While on the visit to his grandparents before alluded to by his mother, he was the picture of health. At that time the miniature was taken which is placed as the frontispiece. The original was painted by F. Agate, who saw the child in Stamford, and who was so struck with his appearance, that he requested the privilege of taking a miniature copy of him. The picture, after having been exhibited in the gallery of paintings in the city of New York, was presented by the artist to Mrs. Boorman, a lady who had shown him some favors in the way of patronage, and who was aunt to the child. In her possession it remained until after his death. It was then kindly sent to his mother by the sympathizing sister, who was among the first to appreciate her nephew's excellences, and who had all along watched with parental solicitude the development of his intellectual, and more especially his moral character.

## CHAPTER II.

### COMMENCEMENT OF HIS CHRISTIAN COURSE.

The year 1832 was distinguished as a season of the remarkable outpouring of the Spirit on the village of Binghamton. During the early part of the fall of that year, and while attending Mrs. B——'s meetings for children, John dated his hope of having passed from death to life. And certainly the events of that period were to him what the transaction recorded in the ninth chapter of the Acts of the Apostles was to Saul, who afterwards was called Paul. Though the antecedent part of his life had not been characterized by breathings out of threatenings and slaughter against the disciples of the Lord, there was, nevertheless, after his supposed conversion, a marked change in his course of conduct. The attitude of the enraged persecutor after his conversion—stretching forth his hands to Jesus, and inquiring with a broken heart and filial submission, "Lord, what wilt thou have me to do?" seems to me to describe the position in which the subject of this memoir should be portrayed, from the period above-named to the time of his death. Other Christians with whom I have been acquainted, and of whom I have read, have had their seasons of declension and of reviving. And though John had undoubtedly his—as he was always, in his prayers, free to confess his unfaithfulness—and though there were seasons observable to others when his heart would seem unusually filled with the graces of the Spirit, I cannot look back on a time in regard to which I should feel myself justified in saying that he *manifested* a lukewarm spirit. And I have reason to believe that all who knew him would be ready cheerfully to unite in this testimony.

From the period above-named, his mental and moral frame seemed not only to receive a new impress, but to take a fresh start in their growth. Though he was younger than any one I had known to make a public profession of religion, he did not seem to be aware of any thing peculiar in his case. He was the same modest, affectionate child as before; and more amiable and obedient to his mother: as cheerful in the family, and as active with his playmates. He was encouraged to be so. His parents and his teacher would have discountenanced it, and grieved if they had seen any approximation to a dull, mopish spirit. For one of his age either to lay aside the sports of youth, or to assume the manners of an adult, they would have considered as unseemly, as it would have been for him to appear dressed in the costume of a full-grown man. When he was a child, his parents loved to see him act and speak as a child; satisfied if, when he became a man, he should put away childish things.

At the time he made a public profession of religion, he was attending a select school in the village, taught by S. W——, a pious young man. He had already, under the tuition of the young lady above referred to, acquired a tolerably accurate knowledge of geography, was well drilled in Colburn's Mental Arithmetic, and "had recited the greater part, if not the whole, of Mrs. B——'s Conversations on Natural Philosophy. While under Miss P——'s tuition, a course of astronomical lectures was delivered in the village. The family attended, and John among the rest. After returning home on one occasion, having been exceedingly interested in the illustration by diagrams, he said to Miss P——, 'I am very much obliged to you for teaching me natural philosophy; for if I had not studied it, I could not have understood half so well the subject of the lecture.'" At Mr. W——'s school, he commenced the study of the Latin and the Greek; and in both these studies made rapid progress.

At that age he used, at our seasons of family worship in the morning, to stand by my side, and read one of Jay's Exercises for the Closet: and the natural, simple, yet expressive style of his reading never failed to arrest the attention of those who heard him. At our family worship on the Sabbath, he not only read in the morning the exercise from Jay, but then, and at evening also, followed his father in prayer. And his prayers on these occasions, though simple and childlike, were nevertheless the effusions of his own heart, and were appropriate. Even at that early age, he thought much about the situation of those who had never heard of the Saviour; and rarely, if ever, failed to remember the heathen in his prayers. This practice of following his father in prayer, at our seasons of family worship on the Sabbath, was continued when both were at home; and to it is perhaps to be attributed, in no small degree, the promptitude with which he was always ready to engage in prayer, and in any public religious exercises.

His heart was early set on being a missionary; and such desires were always carefully and gratefully fostered by his parents. He loved to hear the cause of missions presented. Miss P——, in a letter of condolence to his mother after his death, writes, "How much he used to say, when a very little boy, about being a missionary. Well do I remember his cheerful, happy countenance, his quick and bounding step, as he returned from an evening lecture, having listened to the presentation of the wants and claims of the far west. I seem now to hear his voice exclaiming, 'Mother, if you and I live ten years from this time, I hope you will see me a missionary.'"

Shortly after his death, an early companion

of his, Rev. Silas McKinney, now missionary in Africa, in an affectionate letter of sympathy, relates an interesting fact which illustrates the character of his early piety: "Once, when he was but a child, I remember attending a donation-visit at your own house, and in the levity of the company around us he came to me, and desired me, with one or two other boys, to retire with him to an adjoining room for a season of prayer, as being more suitable to the occasion than the foolish mirth of many about us." This occurred when he was not more than seven and a half years old.

## CHAPTER III.

RESIDENCE IN NEW YORK—IN BINGHAMTON.

The winter of 1833–4 having been spent by his father at Richmond, Virginia, with a view to recruiting his health, John was placed as a pupil in the Washington Institute, New York; and being kindly invited by his aunt, Mrs. B——, to make her house his home, he was in her family and under her care as a son. Frequently has that aunt been heard to say, that during his residence in her family he never in a single instance disobeyed her. The testimony also which his teachers gave from time to time of his deportment in school, and of his proficiency in his studies, was gratifying. But extracts from his own letters will illustrate in the most satisfactory manner the character of his mind, his dutiful and affectionate disposition, and also his standing as a scholar.

In his first letter, dated Nov. 23, 1833, he says, in the simplicity of childhood, being then only a little over eight years of age, "I like the school very much, but mother has not prepared me for boarding yet. If you will tell me that I need not board at the Institute, I shall be very glad: first, because I do not like to go away from my friends; and secondly, because I do not like to sleep in the same room with other boys."

The next is dated the 11th of the succeeding month:

"MY DEAR FATHER—A little before I received your letter, I began to see that it was wrong to ask you to excuse me from boarding at the Institute, and that I ought to sacrifice my will to yours, but I thank you for excusing me. The affairs of my school are, at present, very favorable with me. In my Virgil I am in the Second Book; in my arithmetic, near the fractions; and in my Greek, nearly as far as I have ever been. You must write to me soon; and please tell me if you think I improve in my writing. I am your affectionate son,

"JOHN D. LOCKWOOD."

"NEW YORK, Jan. 14, 1834.

"MY DEAR FATHER—I am very sorry that you have cause to find fault with my writing;

and I hope that you will not have reason to in future, as it will be my endeavor to improve. In reply to your second question, I fear that my spirit of religion is declining; and I do not feel as devoted to God as I wish, or ought to do, or as I did last winter. I pray every morning and evening; and my subjects of prayer are for my parents, and that God would forgive my sins, and make me to grow up and be a useful man. I have found no opportunity of doing good among my school-fellows; but I have the pleasure to inform you that one of them has recently joined the church, a son of Dr. I——. I hoped and thought that you would write to me on the subject of religion, in some of your letters. Now I suppose that you would like to know how I get along in school. My studies are Latin, arithmetic, dictation, writing, and Greek.

"In Latin I have progressed as far as the Second Book of the Æneid, and am reviewing. In arithmetic, I am pretty successful; and am nearly at the head of the class. In dictation, I have been at the head, but am sorry to say that I have gone down to-day. As to my writing, you must judge for yourself; and as to my Greek, I am nearly to the Fables."

"New York, Feb. 17, 1834.

"My dear Father—I was very happy to receive your letter, and to hear that you were well. My missionary box was opened Monday of the same week with New-Year, and two dollars and two or three cents were found in it. I commenced studying French last week; and the reason that I have not attended to it before this winter is, because I thought it would interfere with my other pursuits; but I now find I can attend to it with perfect convenience. I have read a good deal in the Young Christian. I think it is a very excellent book, and intend to read in it frequently. I read a part of the Missionary Herald every month, and feel interested in the missionary intelligence. I very often am tempted to drink tea or coffee; but by the assistance of aunty, or some one else, I am able to resist it, and to persevere in my plan of drinking cold water."

I find only one more directed to me at Richmond, and that is under date of April 26, 1834, in which, after a lapse of more than two months, he thus writes:

"My dear Father—I am very sorry that I have not written to you before, and I fear that you will be very much displeased. The reason that I have not done so before is, that I have not had time. I rise at half past five o'clock, and go to school; and when I get there, go into a cyphering class. After that, I eat breakfast there. Then we have an intermission; and when school goes in, I go into an English parsing class, and go on with my other studies as usual. I learn all my lessons very well, except my Greek: and in that I have fallen off the last few weeks a great deal, but am now a little better in it. I spend my evenings mostly in studying my Latin lesson.

"There has been a great deal of excitement this election, two or three weeks ago. Even the boys seemed to enter into the spirit of it. As I was coming home from school the last day of the election, I was attacked by some of the low rough boys of the city, who asked me if I was for Clay; and then pushed my cap off, and threw me down, and used me very ill. It was with some difficulty that I got away from them.

"I am frequently tried by the laughter of the boys at school, on account of my being a Christian; but I am not ashamed of Christ at any time, though sometimes I am almost overcome by them. I mean to get more to put in my mission-box this year than I did last. I have found again that I cannot attend to French, as that would be loading me with studies. In Sunday-school I am in the second class, and am studying in Acts. I take a great deal of interest in it."

The next winter I opened a classical school in Binghamton, of which John was a member from its commencement; and though among the youngest, he was among the foremost in all his studies, and universally beloved by his companions.

After having been associated in study about eighteen months with those who had taken their departure for college, he was permitted to pursue pretty much his own course, reciting with those who were in classes below him, and occasionally assisting me in teaching the smaller children.

His disposition will appear from one or two incidents which are remembered, as having occurred during this period. At one time when, innocently and from over-eagerness in play, he had been in danger of hurting a younger boy, I called to him with some earnestness; and on his coming to me, said to him, "My dear son, I can't punish you, I know you would not intentionally injure the boy, but you must be careful." John left me, but after a little while returned; and as he took his seat beside me, said, with a sweet and modest expression, as he looked into my face, "Father, you don't know how much good that way of speaking did to me; it did me a great deal more good than if you had whipped me."

One evening, having, for some cause or other which I have now forgotten, found fault with him, I required him to retire to his room without a candle. The next morning early, I found on my study-desk a note, of which the following is a copy:

"DEAR FATHER—I acknowledge that I have done very wrong to-night, and also that I have been in the constant habit of disobeying you. I asked the pardon of *God* last night. Will *you* not forgive me? I will submit to any punishment you think fit, provided you will forgive me.

"Your affectionate son,

"J. D. LOCKWOOD."

The ingenuous confession, and the true spirit of penitence which it manifested, so affected me, that I folded it up, and carefully laid it in my pocket-book, where it has since remained.

On the morning of the 7th of February, 1837, and while in the enjoyment, for aught we knew, of his usual good health, he fell backwards on the floor slightly convulsed, and was, for some time after he was taken up, unconscious. No one was with him but the hired girl of the family. He had unintentionally anticipated by an hour his usual time for rising, and was just expressing his joy at the circumstance, saying to her, "Well, we shall live one hour longer than we otherwise should," when he fell.

Recovering from this attack, however, he

was able to resume his duties as usual; and with encouragement drawn from physicians and others, his friends fondly hoped that the peculiar circumstances of the case might account for this attack, and that there was no reason for apprehending another. His parents, however, were not without much anxiety. On the second of June following, and when the fears of his parents had begun to subside, he was attacked again, while engaged in his mathematical studies in the school-room. It was then settled that the fits were epileptic; and he was immediately taken from his studies, and put under the care of a physician.

On the 11th of August, while on the roof of a building which a carpenter was shingling, he was seized more violently than ever. He had five or six fits in succession.

On the 27th of September, while standing on a back shed of the house, he was again taken; and though he had only three fits at that time, they were peculiarly distressing. At this time, quite a gash was made in his head by his fall against the wheel of a wagon.

After one or two other slight attacks, he had

not another for a year, during which time his father had been stationed in the ministry at Cortlandville, N. Y. Having been so long without any attack, and being strongly desirous to resume his studies, he was permitted to take up his Latin and his algebra. I was astonished and alarmed, however, when I perceived the extent of his lessons. His mind seemed to set off with impetuosity, as if anxious to redeem lost time. I apprized the dear child of my fears, and he did endeavor to be moderate. His lessons seemed to cost him but little effort. On the evening of November 26, 1838, and while sitting with the family with his slate full of algebraical characters on the table before him, the frightful paroxysm again seized him.

As an illustration of the calm and Christian manner in which he regarded this attack, I quote the following from a letter to Miss P——, his first teacher:

"CORTLANDVILLE, Feb. 8, 1839.

"DEAR LOUISA—I think, when I wrote to you last, I was pursuing my studies at home during the evenings; had marked out my plan for the winter, and was getting as much engrossed as ever with my books. But God saw that it was not proper for me to commence study yet; and he therefore gave me a kind and gentle hint to that effect. A day or two after I had been exulting in the thought that I had gone a year without any fits, I was again brought low. But, as I said before, it was a *gentle* admonition; and *very* light, compared with most that I have had. Since that time, I have been careful to take regular exercise every day, and to avoid *all* close attention to any one thing; and I think I have been gaining rapidly. I have sawed all the wood our family has burned this winter."

There is great reason to fear, that under this affliction, as well as others of a similar kind, the son was more calm than his father. I reproached myself for allowing him to touch a book; and the point seemed to be settled in my mind, that much as our hearts were set on seeing our dear son engaged in the ministry, we must relinquish the idea and be satisfied to have him a useful farmer or mechanic.

This determination was made known to him; and it is affecting to recall the docility and submission with which he received it. It must have been to him a sore disappointment. He had such a thirst for useful knowledge, such a desire for imparting instruction, such a passion for doing good. During the winter he spent in Binghamton, he had been led to fear that such might be the result at which his parents would be forced to arrive; and one of the deacons in the church being an ingenious mechanic, he used regularly to visit his shop and endeavor to get some knowledge of machinery, and some instruction in the use of tools. In the course of that winter he made several fancy articles, and among the rest a stand for the younger children, which has been in use in the family ever since. That same winter he taught, in my school-room, the children of a neighbor's family, being strongly urged to do it by their mother.

In a letter to one of his cousins in New York, dated January 17, 1838, I find the following allusion to this subject: "A gentleman by the name of W—— has lately moved into the neighborhood. There are no good schools here; and as Mrs. W—— did not wish her boys to associate with those they would find in the village, she desired me to instruct them. They accordingly come over into father's school-room, where I set them lessons and hear them recite, or in other words, '*keep school.*' I endeavor to open and close the school as a Christian should, with prayer."

In this same letter pleasing evidence is also furnished of his love for souls. He thus inquires about another cousin, who was not at that time, as he is now, a professor of religion: "Do you know how dear William feels on the subject of religion? Is he any more anxious about the salvation of his soul than he has been hitherto? I intend to write to him by this opportunity, if I have time. I pray for him every night and morning, and sometimes have had blessed seasons in pleading for him at the throne of grace." And then turning to his correspondent, his senior in age and a professor of religion, he thus continues: "And now, dear George, permit me to ask, How is your spiritual health? Those resolutions of James Brainerd Taylor, which you referred to, are very good ones. He is the only one that I remember who went through college unharmed by its polluting touch. May you be another one, and may you be *much farther* advanced in the divine life after having gone through college, than you were when you entered. I hope that you do exert a heavenly influence around you, and may be the means of doing great good in the station which Providence has allotted to you. I should think there was a great field for usefulness in college; and you may, if you try, be the means of leading many souls to the fold of Christ. I pray for you every day, as I expect you do for me: and O, may we both become, as J. B. Taylor expresses it, "uncommon Christians;" may we live *near the throne* of grace; may we become ornaments to the ministry, if we shall be permitted to enter it; and may we at last meet in heaven to *dwell with Christ*, FOR EVER. It will be two months on Friday since I have had a fit, and I hope that the means now in use may entirely remove my disease. I hope you will pray not only for my recovery, but also that I may be resigned to God's will concerning me.

"Your affectionate cousin, J. D. L."

That winter he first asked a blessing at the table during his mother's absence. In a letter to me at Cortland, dated Dec. 20, 1837, he thus alludes to the circumstance: "Last evening, and this evening also, mother has been away from supper. And the first time H——," a young man residing in the family, "asked the blessing; but the last time *he* was away. As I knew I should have to take up the cross some time or other, I broke the ice. Although I did not succeed as well as I wished, I think it must have been from this cause that R—— has behaved himself much better than he generally does when mother is absent."

With his cousin George he had exchanged several letters prior to the above; and in each the case of William is introduced in a way to show that for several years he had made his conversion a special subject of prayer to God. Under date of Nov. 4, 1835, when he was a little over ten years of age, he thus writes:

"DEAR GEORGE—"I often feel the want of a companion with whom I can be familiar. I find that it is a good plan when I retire at night to pray, to ask myself the question, Have I this day done any thing for the glory of God? Nearly every night that I have applied this question, I have been compelled to answer in the negative.

"I should like to know how William feels on the subject of religion. I am longing to catch the good news that he is converted. I pray for him every night and morning, and hope that the day is not far distant when he will be trusting in God."

In the next he writes, "William has now entered upon a scene where he will be exposed to many temptations; and how much grace should he have to resist them. Let us wrestle with God in prayer—take hold of his promises and cling to them, and he will assuredly grant us the blessing."

Later still—May 20, 1837—he thus writes:

"Dear George—Cousin William's accident ought to remind us of the uncertainty of life. I hope that this accident—Oh, that it may not be in the end a misfortune—will be blessed to his good. Now, perhaps, it would be as fit a time as any to present before him the subject—the worth of his soul. I wrote a letter to him on that subject this spring. But I found that all my powers were too feeble to express the danger there would be in rejecting Christ, and the happiness of following him. If it is possible for you, I wish you would go over to Brooklyn and talk with him upon this all-important subject. In this way you might be the means of saving his soul. If this affliction be indeed blessed to the salvation of his soul, as I humbly hope and pray it may, we shall both of us have double the amount of happiness in his company that we had before.

"You speak of your intention to study for the ministry. I am glad you have come to that resolution. It has been my design to be a minister nearly ever since I entertained a hope. I expect, Providence permitting, to be a missionary to China; and how pleasant it would be for us both to be ministering to the spiritual wants of that nation. Perhaps you have already fixed upon your future sphere of labor. If you have *not*, may I ask you if you will direct your thoughts thither? But if you have, I do not mean to divert your attention from it, by any means. I lately took up 'Henry Martyn,' and was peculiarly impressed with the thought, if so good a man as he speaks in such abasing terms of himself, how ought I to be humbled in the dust."

In a subsequent letter to the same, he writes, "Have there been any conversions in college lately? Is there a good state of feeling there? And how is your own mind? I think that we who expect to become ministers of the gospel, ought to be peculiarly careful to set a good example before the world. And we ought to be faithful to our companions, in order to prepare us for the faithful discharge of our future duties. I know I do not perform my duty as I should. The fear of man, that detestable, time-serving spirit, is a great drawback to the Christian; but it ought to be overcome."

During this last winter of his residence in Binghamton, he drew up the following document; which, after his death, was found in his drawer, among his papers, filed, and labelled, "Self-consecration:"

"BINGHAMTON, Jan. 1, 1838.

"As I am now commencing a new year, it is important that I should commence it aright. And, in my opinion, the proper way is, in praising God for the mercies of the past year, in repenting of the sins which have been committed, and in forming resolutions to live more to the glory of God during the year to come.

"In reviewing the past year, I find that although my health has not been as good as on some former years, yet it has been not worse than I deserve; and I have great reason to bless the Lord that I have enjoyed such a measure of health as I have, while others have been racked with pain; and in circumstances, too, that have rendered it doubly painful. I have suffered but very little, bodily; and have been blessed with a comfortable home, kind friends, and a thousand other mercies, which God is continually showering down upon me. It is certainly true of me, if of any one, that in the midst of affliction God has remembered mercy. And I can say with the psalmist, 'What shall I render unto the Lord for all his benefits towards me?'

"I have also to bless the Lord for spiritual

as well as temporal benefits. I think I can truly say, that during the past year I have grown in grace more than in any year previous. I bless and praise God that he has preserved me from falling, in all my wanderings; and has given me grace to make those advances in divine life which I have.

"But while I praise God for his goodness to me, it becomes me to repent, and to humble myself in dust and ashes on account of my sins. My sins have been many and aggravated. I have oftentimes wandered from the fold of Christ; and have, times and ways without number, disgraced the religion I profess, both by sins of omission and of commission. My daily walk and conversation has not been such as becomes a disciple of the meek and lowly Jesus. And I fear that my example has done a great injury to the cause of Christ: how much the judgment-day only will show.

"And now, Lord, I humbly beseech thee to pardon all my sins and forgive my iniquities. Oh, blot them out of the book of thy remembrance; and may they no longer be remembered before thee. I now, on the first day of the new year, consecrate myself anew to thy service. If it should please thee to restore my health entirely, and to preserve me from any more attacks of my disease, my life shall be entirely devoted to thy service. But if it is not consistent with thy will, Oh Lord, I beseech thee that I may be prepared for whatever is preparing for me. And I do now resolve, God helping me, that in whatever circumstances I am placed, I will hereafter endeavor to do more for thy glory and the good of souls than I have hitherto done. Dear Saviour, I do now beseech thee to enable me to keep these resolutions, and to become an *uncommon* Christian. And finally, when thou hast done serving thyself with me here below, may I be received into the heavenly mansions, for the Redeemer's sake. Amen."

A pious lady in Binghamton recently portrayed to me one of his exemplary traits, as a member of the Sabbath-school in Binghamton. "He always appeared in school with his lesson well studied. And when, as at that time was frequently the case, some point of supposed difficulty in the lesson would be raised by the superintendent in order to elicit the energies of the school, John, though but a child, would frequently be seen to arise, and with modesty would say, in reference to the point in question, 'Dr. Scott in his Commentary says, thus and so; Matthew Henry, in his Exposition, expresses this opinion; or, Adam Clarke thinks, thus.' "

At this time the Sunday-school was organized, as far as practicable, into a Juvenile Missionary Society. Its meetings were held at every Sunday-school monthly concert. At which time the congregation would listen to an address from one of the members, previously designated for that purpose. Among John's papers recently found, are two addresses for the Sunday-school Missionary Society, Binghamton. One, delivered by him Dec. 12, 1836, or when he was eleven years and two months old. The other, March 12, 1838, fifteen months after.

The direct object of the society was, to procure funds sufficient to sustain heathen children in the mission schools at Batticotta and

Oodooville, Ceylon. One year the society sustained four children, though ordinarily they sustained only two.

The subject of his first juvenile lecture is, The Ceylon Mission. "This mission," he says, "at the present time is in a very prosperous condition, and has encouraging prospects. The first missionaries from the American Board to Ceylon sailed Oct. 23, 1815, taking with them a printing-press; and soon after their arrival commenced schools for the children, in one of which there were soon sixteen boys able to read the Tamul and English Testament easily. In 1817, the prospects of the mission were very flattering. Although the number of schools at Ceylon was less than it was in Bombay, yet the system of instructing children and youth was promising much good. At Batticotta, Oodooville, Tillipally, and several other places on the island, there has recently been an outpouring of the Spirit. The whole number of admissions to the church in March, 1835, was fifty-one; of these, thirty-nine belonged to the different schools.

"There are three things which will be the

principal instruments in the hand of God of bringing about this great work: these three things are men, money, and prayer. Now if these great instruments moved together, that is, if the treasury was full at the same time that many pious and devoted men were ready and willing to go, and the people of God were zealous and frequent in prayer for this cause, the great work of converting the world would soon be accomplished. But this is not so. At one time there has been an abundance of money, while there were few or none ready to go as missionaries. At another time, as is the case now, the missions abroad are in a very prosperous state, and there are upwards of fifty missionaries wishing to go as soon as the means are afforded; but the treasury is empty: there is a debt of several thousand dollars, which the society have already contracted, and the expenses of the new missionaries will probably swell the debt to $100,000. Now, by whom is this great debt to be paid? True, the cities will probably do a great deal of the work; several have already given largely towards liquidating the debt; but they cannot, and they will not do the whole, for it would not be proper to lay the whole burden upon them. The villages and towns in our country are to help forward the payment of this debt very much. But are there not some other means which, although they cannot accomplish as much as cities and villages, can yet help a little? Yes, blessed be God, there are the Sunday-school missionary societies. And among these may not the Binghamton Sunday-school Missionary Society be permitted to hold a place? Yes, this humble society may be the instrument in the hands of God of doing much good. But while we are thus laboring for the conversion of the heathen by contributing of our substance, should we not also pray for it? Many persons will probably see children in heaven whom they never saw before—the fruit of their prayers: and how glorious will be their crown of rejoicing. But what tongue can tell the feelings of those who in hell behold heathen children who have been exalted to heaven by their means? How bitterly will they reflect on the hours they spent in this place, giving money for the conversion of heathen, while they themselves were far from the kingdom. I apprehend that there are not a few members of this society who are in this state, and some influential members too. To such I would say, 'Flee from the wrath to come. Remember, that if you die, what repenting, what bitter anguish will wring your heart when you think of the opportunities you have let pass for giving up your heart to God.' To those who have already given themselves to God, I would say, 'Persevere to the end. Give, and pray, and if it seem to be your duty, give even yourself for this work. Your crown of rejoicing will be glorious indeed, filled with many stars as trophies of your labor.'"

The other address gives a general view of the principal missionary stations under the care of the American Board; and closes, like the first, with an appeal to different classes of his hearers. The handwriting of a part of this address is beautiful. As a specimen of its style and spirit, the following is given from the introduction and the close. Both addresses evince an accurate knowledge of the existing state of the heathen world, and of missions; the fruit, undoubtedly, of his intimate acquaintance with the Missionary Herald: and both were long remembered with peculiar interest by the superintendent and others who heard them. The last was delivered only a few weeks prior to his departure for Cortland:

"My young friends, members of this association, you are engaged in a noble enterprise; one which may involve the interests of immortal souls throughout eternity. If the effort should terminate merely in the conversion of your beneficiaries, yet if the salvation of one soul is a theme worthy of the admiration and joy of all heaven, it certainly is worth the noblest energies of man to be the means of bringing that one soul from the darkness of sin to the marvellous light of the gospel. But the result will not stop here. We are encouraged by God's promises to believe that they will become Christians; and if they do, the spirit of the gospel will lead them to devise some way of doing good to their benighted countrymen. They may become ministers of the gospel; and through their instrumentality, hundreds and perhaps thousands may be brought to give up their idolatrous practices, and worship the only true God and Jesus Christ whom he has sent.

"Nor will the reward of your benevolence end here. They in turn will seek to communicate to others the blessing they have received; and thus, through the aid of the individual contributions of *every one* engaged in this cause, a train of events will be set in motion, which will go on, continually making new accessions to the Redeemer's kingdom, through every successive generation till the end of time. How glorious the thought! Not one, nor ten, nor one hundred, but thousands, singing eternal praises to the Lamb who has purchased their pardon. Oh, my friends, if you could bring your whole mind to bear upon this subject, you would be lost in raptures; and would be induced to redouble your exertions, and renew your sacrifices, in order to the accomplishment of this blessed object."

Then follows the body of the address. After which he proceeds, in conclusion,

"You, my young friends, are placed in a

situation fraught with advantages. You are permitted to come up to the house of God every Sunday, and to study his holy word. And this talent which has been given to you is not to be squandered away, nor even to be laid up in a napkin; but is to be used for the honor and glory of the giver. You ought to carry out into the week, and practise the truths which you have learnt on the Sabbath. You ought to show, by your daily walk and conversation, that they have had some effect upon the heart.

"Those of you who are members of the church, and especially the young converts, are at the present time placed in peculiarly trying circumstances. You are about to lose your spiritual shepherd; and several of your young Christian friends intend soon to leave you. It will be necessary for you to put on the whole armor of God, and to be instant in prayer. Secret prayer is an excellent remedy for worldly-mindedness. And it will generally be found, that when the fervor of a Christian remains unabated in his morning and evening devotions, the same spirit will pervade all the business of the day. Prayer is, of all things, best calculated to keep the Christian armor bright. The closet is the place where Jesus appears sweetest to the believer. Keep up also the *social* prayer-meetings. Let every one feel as if it were his duty to go *himself*, and make the meetings as interesting as he can. Social intercourse is another great advantage to the Christian. Wherever you meet, make religion the principal theme. Tell each other your troubles, and advise concerning them. And whatever else you do, do not neglect to converse with impenitent sinners. Warn them of their danger. Pray ardently for their salvation; and endeavor by every means in your power, to persuade them to come to Jesus.

"In conclusion, I will say a few words to my impenitent friends. Although you are now at peace, rest assured it is but a false security, which is the prelude to destruction. It will be soon, very soon, at the farthest, when you will lie on the bed of death. And *then*, although *now* it appears horrible even to think of eternal things, you will be obliged to look into the grave; and if still impenitent, yet farther, into the lake which burns with fire and brimstone, and see the inexpressible torments which await you there.

"Still more terrible, if possible, will be your feelings when you come before the judgment-seat of Christ:

'That awful day will surely come,
The appointed hour makes haste,
When you must stand before the Judge,
And pass the solemn test.'

Then repentance will be too late. Looking around, you will discover your parents and dear friends on the right hand; while you, who despised all their prayers and entreaties when alive, are now entirely out of the reach of mercy. Soon, the Judge will pronounce those terrible words, 'Depart, ye cursed, into everlasting fire, prepared for the devil and his angels.' And you will be confined in the prison-house of despair, there to remain with devils and lost spirits *for ever!* FOR EVER!! FOR EVER!!!

"And now, to all—Farewell. This is probably the last opportunity I shall have of meeting you on an occasion like this. But I shall ever remember with the liveliest emotions of gratitude and pleasure, the *many* happy hours I have spent here.

"I shall always remember you all in my prayers; especially the Sunday-school, and my Christian friends here. And I request that they would bear me in their petitions at the throne of grace. And O, may we all, when we come to the last great day, be found among that great multitude which no man can number, of all nations and kindred, and people and tongues, of whom it is said, 'They stood before the throne and before the Lamb, clothed with white robes, and palms in their hands; and cried with a loud voice, Salvation be to our God, which sitteth upon the throne, and to the Lamb.'"

## CHAPTER IV.

### RESIDENCE IN CORTLANDVILLE.

AFTER the attack already alluded to, on the the evening of the 26th Nov., 1838, under the impression that his mind had been acquiring growth and strength at the expense of his physical constitution, it was recommended that he should remain about home, engaging in any light business in which his services might be wanted—on a farm, in a shop, or in a store; in other words, to suffer his mind to rest for a few years.

In this recommendation he cheerfully acquiesced. And during the time the family lived in Cortland, he sawed and split our wood, made the garden, and did similar work. Besides this, he went into the workshop; learned the art of bottoming chairs with rushes; acted one season as clerk in a store. And in these ways, and by aiding neighbors on the farm during harvest, he not only benefited his health, but acquired funds enough to contribute to all the benevolent operations of the day.

His uncle in New York having about this time presented him with a gentleman's chest of tools, he fixed up a work-bench, at one time in the barn, at another over the wood-house, where he employed his leisure hours in making toys for his younger sisters, or flower-pots, as presents for his friends. Though leading at this time a mode of life which was so desultory, and so repugnant to his natural disposition, *he was never idle*, and *seldom* was he dejected. For a few days after the occurrence of one of his attacks, he would be pensive and rather dull. At other times he was habitually cheerful; and his presence was the delight of the family.

About a year after he came to live in Cortland, the superintendent of the Sunday-school appointed him teacher of a class of boys, averaging from ten to twelve years of age. Some of them *he* gathered into the school. With this class, John was faithful; not only instructing them on the Sabbath, furnishing them with suitable books from the Sunday-school library, and loaning them his own books to carry home with them, but he visited them regularly at their houses, and thus made himself acquainted with their parents as well as themselves. Thus he succeeded in ingratiating himself into the good will of these families. The father of one of the lads was intemperate. But, even while intoxicated, he would listen to the voice of this youthful teacher of his son, when he would only vent his rage at others who were attempting to control or to influence him.

His views on the subject of temperance were well known. While he was acting as clerk in the store of Mr. R——, a lad came in with a jug, to be filled with liquor for the workmen. "John," said Mr. R——, "just take that jug and fill it." "I can't do that, sir," was the prompt but mild reply. And, as Mr. R—— informs me, he himself, respecting John's scruples, took the jug and filled it.

In October, 1836, while a pupil in my school in Binghamton, he commenced keeping a journal of the temperature, and of the weather. And for nearly five years he was in the habit of furnishing for the newspaper of the villages in which he lived, a weekly meteorological table. A copy of his observations, made three times a day during the period named above, is found laid aside among his papers.

The time when he commenced asking a blessing at the table has been already noted. In the summer of 1839 he commenced conducting family worship during the absence of his parents. And this practice he continued ever after. Both these exercises he undertook without any suggestion from his parents, entirely of his own accord, and actuated by a sense of propriety and duty.

During the time of his residence in Cortland, he was actively engaged in endeavoring to do good in the church, and especially among the youth of that village. A veil must, for the present, be thrown over some of these efforts among his fellow-youths. Suffice it to say, the ardent desires of his soul for their salvation were not appreciated by some; and the publication of the correspondence with such, though it would not alter the state of the dead, might wound the feelings of the living.

In January, 1841, however, the fruit of his labors and prayers began to appear. Towards the close of the preceding year, the church had become evidently revived; but on the evening of the second Sabbath of the new year a thrilling scene occurred in the vestry of the church, where the congregation were accustomed to assemble to hold their third service—a social conference and prayer-meeting. At this meeting the pastor was accustomed to preside. On the occasion above alluded to, and while before a breathless audience the pastor was describing the situation of a sinner—condemned already, in the dark prison, with a pardon offered him, and the folly and the guilt of such a one shrinking back and declining to receive the pardon—one of the young men of the village, tall in stature, and occupying a position in a remote part of the room, rose on his feet, and drawing towards him the attention of all as he cried out with a tremulous voice, "That's me! That's me! I can't stand it any longer"—left his place, and threading his way through the pent-up passages, came to the speaker's table; and there, throwing himself on his knees, exclaimed, "Oh, pray for *me!* pray for *me!* or is it too late?—O, my Sabbath-school! O, my pious mother!—I have put it off too long already." In expressions like these, he continued for some minutes to give vent to his troubled feelings: after which, the congregation were requested to unite with their pastor in fervent prayers to God in behalf of this young friend.

This was the sudden commencement of a revival of religion among the young men. As the fruits of which, twenty-five of this interesting class were added to the Presbyterian church from the world; and with them twenty females.

As the means in the hands of God of effecting this desirable change in the hearts of these precious youths, I have always looked upon John's faithful conversation, consistent life, and fervent prayers, as bearing a conspicuous part. There was nothing boisterous or obtrusive in his manner. His influence was like the gentle dew.

And now that a band of new recruits had come into the church, he endeavored to enlist them in doing good to others. On this topic he would dwell in his conversations with them, and in his addresses at their social meetings.

Among his papers I find one which appears to be the copy of "a note" addressed "to William Stimson," one of the young converts, dated "Feb. 19, 1841," and is as follows: "Please look at Leviticus 19 : 17; Proverbs 24 : 11, 12; 25 : 11; 11 : 30; 15 : 7, 23; Matthew 5 : 13–16; Heb. 13 : 16; Jas. 3 : 13; 5 : 20. If it were necessary, I could probably refer you to as many more passages on the same subject. But I think these will be sufficient to prove that we all have a *duty* to perform, in warning impenitent sinners. For here are some passages, in which there is a positive command; as well as others, in which the practice is recommended, and promises made to those who perform this duty. And when it is once proved to be a *duty*, you know, the sooner its performance, the better."

The individual to whom this note was addressed, commenced studying for the ministry; but on account of ill health was obliged to desist, and has since died.

From John's journal under date of Dec. 15, 1840, I quote as follows: "Evening, went to singing-school. In recess had a short conversation with William Stimson on the subject of religion. Commenced with hesitation and trembling; but before we finished, he asked me to pray for him. I cheerfully complied, and endeavored to urge upon him the importance of making an effort to pray for himself. May it not be that the harps of angels shall soon be tuned to welcome the return of this dear youth. He says he has been for three or four years in just about the same situation he is now."

A young lady of Cortland reminds me of the following incident, which occurred about this time. The revival was, as usual, followed by strenuous efforts on the part of the irreligious, to create a reaction in favor of vain amusements. A series of cotillion parties was announced and commenced. The parties would frequently, and I do not know but invariably, occur on the same evening with the young people's prayer-meeting. On one occasion of this sort, when a good deal of solicitude was felt for certain individuals who that evening were placed in circumstances of temptation, John arose in the meeting and remarked to this effect: he feared they had not been faithful with certain individuals; he feared they had not labored enough with them; and now it is too late. He feared they had not prayed to God enough for them; and perhaps it is not too late yet—let us pray. He then commenced praying in view of the specific case. His feelings became more fervent as he proceeded; and when he closed, another, having caught the same spirit, commenced. Another succeeded him, and a remarkable spirit of prayer pervaded the meeting. The next morning, to their surprise, they ascertained that the party the evening before could not succeed in "making out a single figure." Not one cotillion was danced. In consequence of some unexpected occurrences, not more than six ladies could be induced to go into the room, and the attempt that evening was a complete failure. This was known among the band of praying young converts, and it tended greatly to strengthen within them their belief in the efficacy of prayer.

The following letters, written about this time to a young man in Binghamton, show that though his residence was removed from that village, he had not forgotten the cause of Christ there. They also furnish another proof, in addition to those already adduced, not only that he was accustomed to make particular individuals special subjects of prayer, but that when this is done heartily and perseveringly, God often manifests his approbation by granting the blessing asked for:

"CORTLANDVILLE, Oct. 10, 1840.

"DEAR THEODORE—Deacon Smith of Binghamton has communicated to me the joyful intelligence of your hopeful conversion. Ever since I have lived here, I have been interested in your behalf. Why it is, I know not. But I think it is for this reason: I knew that you did, a few years ago, indulge the hope that you were a Christian; that you lost that hope, and passed through a powerful revival the following fall without regaining it. And I knew also that if you should die in that state, your guilt would be a thousand-fold greater than if you never had come out of the world.

"That spring, you may remember, we knelt side by side in the prayer-meeting; and it was natural that I should feel anxious for your salvation.

"Since I have lived here, I have made it my practice to present you daily in prayer to God, that you might be converted. When I learned that there was a revival in progress in Binghamton, I was very desirous that you should be a subject of it. I even commenced a letter to you, but for some reason did not finish it. And I have not been able to gain any intelligence respecting you since, until this week. I was, as you may suppose, *very much rejoiced;* and, I think, truly grateful, that God had answered my prayers.

"And now I will submit it for your serious consideration, whether it is your duty to study for the ministry. It seems to me, that whenever a young man becomes hopefully pious, this is a question which deserves the prayerful and deliberate exercise of his best judgment; and that it should not be turned off until the inducements on both sides have been thoroughly examined, and the aid of some suitable religious friend and counsellor obtained. There are many things to be considered on both sides.

But unless there is some insurmountable obstacle in the way, that person assumes a fearful responsibility who turns a deaf ear to the wants of perishing millions, in this land and in other lands. On every side the demand is coming for more men.

"I hope you will receive this letter, as I trust it has been written, in the spirit of kindness. My apology for writing is, that I wished to inform you that there was one heart on earth, of which perhaps you did not know, that united with the angels in heaven in rejoicing over the repenting prodigal.

"Your affectionate friend,

"J. D. L."

The individual thus addressed did not at once make a public profession of religion. And in the spring of 1841 he received a friendly appeal, of which the following is an extract; from which it appears that he had previously been conversed with by John on the subject:

"CORTLANDVILLE, April 24, 1841.

"DEAR THEODORE—Perhaps it would be superfluous for me to address you on the subject of uniting with the church; but as father is going down next week, I have concluded to send a line by him.

"Another communion-season will soon come round. And it must be, that the question has been agitated in your mind, whether you will come out on the first Sabbath in May, and make a public profession of religion.

"I will simply bring up two arguments, which, it seems to me, upon a careful consideration must appear reasonable. I have had occasion this winter to observe something of the workings of the human mind, as it has been a very favorable time for that object. I speak now particularly with reference to those who have obtained hope. Several of them have been at times in the same situation that I fear you are, or at least were when I last had the privilege of seeing you—rather desponding, taking no enjoyment in religion, and performing Christian duties rather as a task than as a privilege. As I had been a professor of religion longer than any of them, they would often come to me to know what was the matter. And on looking into the cases, I have *most commonly found that their state of feeling was caused by the neglect of some duty.*

"I think it may safely be laid down as a proposition, that if a Christian neglects a duty that is clearly made known to him, it will bring leanness into his soul. I have found it so in my own experience, as well as in that of others. Now, may it not be that your neglect of this important duty has been the principal, if not the only cause of your troubled state of mind? If it is, and I hardly think you will fail of finding it to be so, then come out on the next Sabbath and remove that cause. Understand me, I do not wish you to perform any duty *for the sake of being happy*. *That* would be as contrary to *my* principles as to *yours*. But do it as you once told me you performed the common daily duties of the Christian—because it is a duty.

"Did you ever see a plant that had grown in the dark—for instance, in a cellar—through the winter? If you have, you will understand the force of my second argument. You have noticed how pale and sickly it looks; how it turns towards the light, whenever a ray enters the place, as if longing to feel its influence, and yet debarred by its situation from the blessing. Such a plant can never become strong, vigorous, and healthy, while remaining in the dark. Neither, as I apprehend, can a Christian become a strong, vigorous, and healthy one, while remaining in the cold and dark world. He will always be sickly. Doubts and fears will harass him. He will be deprived of the counsel, sympathy, and encouragement of many, who otherwise would be of much assistance to him. He will be debarred, by his own feelings, from many of the privileges which he might enjoy. In short, although he may look for, and bend towards every ray of Christian light that may reach him, yet he can never enjoy the full blaze of the sunshine of his Saviour's countenance, while remaining, as far as any public profession is concerned, in the ranks of his enemies.

"I would not on any account have you think that I write these lines with any thing of an assuming or dictatorial spirit. On the contrary, it is merely as a friend, and, I trust, a Christian brother, that I write to you. And I hope that if *my arguments* have no weight, your own reflection will decide that your best, and indeed your only course, if you wish to be a useful Christian, is, to unite yourself with the people of God. I should like to hear how that prayer-meeting gets along at Mr. D——'s.

"Your affectionate friend,

"J. D. L."

John never forgot "the Binghamton Juvenile Missionary Society." For some time after his removal to Cortland, he continued his regular subscription to its funds. Several times, in visiting Binghamton, he endeavored to make his arrangements so as to meet with them on the evening of the third Monday of the month. And generally, if not invariably, would embrace the opportunity given of addressing his young associates.

It had been his ardent desire to see such an association established in Cortland. And after the revival there in the winter of 1841, the young men came forward, and by giving a new shape to the missionary association which was already in existence among the females, communicated to it an impulse, the effect of which was visible for years afterwards.

While in Cortland, he grew rapidly in bodily stature and bodily strength. And as his physical constitution improved, his fits gradually became both less violent and less frequent. In the year 1839, he had two in the spring; one of them pretty severe. In the year 1840, three; all of them light. With the opening spring of 1842 our hopes were becoming sanguine that he had passed, or with due care would soon pass beyond the reach of danger from these dreadful and insidious attacks. By this time, John began to feel as if he had arrived at an age when he ought to be turning his attention to some one employment which he might safely follow, and in which he might continue till the close of life. Supposing that it might be safest for him to follow an agricultural life, and yielding to other providential indications, I relinquished my charge in the village of Cortland, and in the month of June accepted of an invitation to take the pastoral care of a congregation of respectable farmers, in the retired and beautiful valley of Berkshire, distant twenty-two miles from Cortland, and twenty-six miles north-west from Binghamton.

## CHAPTER V.

### RESIDENCE IN BERKSHIRE—IN HOMER.

The year 1842 passed without any symptoms of the old disorder. In the fall of that year he was invited by the trustees to teach a district school in the neighborhood, during the winter. And as he appeared inclined to try the experiment, his parents with some hesitation gave their consent.

In a letter to a brother in New York, he writes, under date of Oct. 7, 1842, "Please tell our city friends that farming looks better in the distance, than it does when you are fairly engaged in it; as some of those who have left the city to try it, find to their sorrow.

"I have been at work for Mr. M—— some, lately. But I find that digging potatoes and rolling logs are occupations not very well calculated to make a good writer; as this letter will show. I think some of teaching school this winter. If I do, I shall probably improve my handwriting at any rate. I could do nothing on a farm in the winter, and teaching is the only other employment I can find. I know not how I shall like it; but I think I shall try, as I must do it, or stay at home and do nothing."

In another letter to the same, dated Nov. 28, he gives the following rather amusing account of his first days in his new employment: "I have taken the school that I was thinking of when I last wrote; and I cannot give you a better idea of my situation than by reviewing the three weeks that I have passed in it. I need not tell you of the resolutions I made to persevere to the last; of my plans of managing my school; of the model which I was going to form for all succeeding school-teachers to study; of my working out some of the hardest sums in the arithmetic, for fear some of my scholars would puzzle me; nor, finally, of my being nonplussed when I was inspected—in parsing a sentence, of which I understood the philosophy as well as the inspectors, and perhaps better, and which I could have parsed well enough if it had been Latin or Greek.

"I pass over all these, and come to the time

when I took charge of a motley set of boys and girls—some pretty well advanced in their studies, and some who scarcely knew any thing; with different kinds of books, and some with no books.

"The first day I felt very much relieved when school was out, though when I looked forward to four months of it, it saddened me some. However, I found it very pleasant where I boarded the first fortnight; and went at it again the next day. But next day it was worse; and Wednesday afternoon, after school was out, I felt as if I should sink into the earth; but I sustained myself by all the consolations within my reach. And, believe me, R——, there is nothing like a trust in Christ at such times; and for the rest of the week, I had comparatively little trouble. The next week, however, a couple of boys came in, whose very countenances showed me that I should have trouble with them. Monday was a complete scene of confusion, all day; and Tuesday was worse. I had not yet used my ruler at all. In my *model* I had expected to govern by mild measures. Tuesday morning I made quite a speech to my scholars, and told them that if they would not behave themselves without it, I *must* take the ruler. But I did nothing that day; and at night, as soon as school was out, I started for home with as complete an idea of Bedlam in my head as I ever want to have. I was completely discouraged, and on the point of giving up.

"After tea, I was sitting by the fire in no very pleasant mood, when the door opened, and who should come in but Dr. G——, from Cortlandville. I started from my chair in surprise. I knew he would say something to refresh me. He told me I must pull my own hair, and put on a good plaster of courage, and go to work; tear around, and put some life into the school, and not sit down brooding over my troubles. So, to work I went the next morning; feruled some, turned others out of doors, and gave knocks over the shoulders by the wholesale. I felt rather better that night: and, since then, I have not been so far gone; though I have sometimes been a good deal tried and worried.

"But say, Aunt R—— and Aunt B——, and my other good friends in the city, how has your health been all this time? Health! I have had no time to think of it. I have eaten any thing that I could get, and my system has been as regular as it could be. You must know, in explanation of my remark as to what I eat, that I board around among the families, so many days for a scholar.

"I have not said half I want to; and almost regret I had not taken a foolscap sheet. I could give you some queer pictures of real life, had I only the ability.

"Your affectionate brother,

"J. D. L."

The school-house was pleasantly situated, about three quarters of a mile from our place of residence. And as John knew nothing by experience of the manner in which district schools were ordinarily conducted, having never in his life been a member of such a school, his mother, aware that he would meet with unexpected trials, and fearful of the effect they might have on his nervous system, proposed to him, that instead of boarding around among the families, as teachers were accustomed to, he should board at home. But the idea did not find favor with John. Dearly as he loved home, he loved still more the idea of doing good. Most of the families belonged to my congregation. And with these he thought he should become better acquainted; and a temporary residence in their families would be both pleasant and profitable to all. He hoped also—and this appeared to be his principal motive—that he might do good, *wherever* he boarded. At all events, he would become somewhat acquainted with the world; see how farmers in the country lived; and as he was expecting one day or other to launch out, this would be a good opportunity to begin to push off his bark. And accordingly, as other teachers had been in the habit of doing, he boarded in the different families in the district.

In this way, it is believed, he exerted a good influence on the parents as well as on the children. Sometimes it was his lot to board where no family altar was reared. And in such cases, while I have never heard of his being rude or obtrusive, he invariably secured from the head of the family an invitation to conduct family worship while he remained with them.

Indeed, having at that time always been accustomed to live where that reasonable and truly Christian duty was performed, he felt as if it was an indispensable part of living.

It is moreover believed that the judgment-day will reveal good, that has resulted from this humble effort to introduce prayer into certain families.

On closing his school in the spring, his constitution seemed so much invigorated that he gained the consent of his parents to try the effect of moderate study once more. Medical advisers encouraged us to think there would be no harm in his doing so, provided he would apply his mind in moderation.

In April, 1843, he took his leave of us for Homer, situated two miles north of Cortlandville; and taking board and lodgings in the family of Dr. Bradford, became a pupil in the deservedly celebrated academy in that pleasant village. Now he was in his element. From his journal it appears that he enjoyed his situation highly. Fond as he was of mental application, he did not confine himself closely to his studies; but having a circle of acquaintance in the vicinity, he visited a good deal. He also *botanized* some; and, for the sake of the vigorous bodily exercise it afforded him, sawed wood; and after having demolished the doctor's woodpile, requested of Mr. Woolworth the principal, who lived nearly opposite, the privilege of attacking his. "It was interesting," says Mr. Woolworth, "as an illustration of his habits of order, to see how punctually he would come, every morning, and how regularly he would leave, after having sawed his usual quantity."

Every stated religious meeting of the scholars he not only attended, but was forward to sustain. Every day he seemed to consider lost, in which he had not made some active efforts to do good. As an illustration of his spirit, I quote from his journal, under date of Saturday, May 6: "Have been helping Mr. Nelson plant a tree on the grave of Abel F. Kinney, formerly teacher of languages in this academy, and a devotedly pious man. Mr. Nelson wished the motto had been put upon his tombstone, 'He went about doing good;' and it would truly have expressed his character. It appears to me, that to deserve such a motto on my tombstone, I would forego any thing that this world can give. Let me daily search my heart, and pray God to see if ambition lodges there. Let me daily strive for more holiness, and daily seek opportunities for doing good." Constantly was he watching for occasions to benefit his fellow-students; encouraging and stimulating his young brethren, as well as kindly exhorting the impenitent.

Not content with doing good in his ordinary walks, he in connection with another individual commenced a Sabbath-school, about four miles from the village, in the north-west part of the town. This distance they used to walk after attending public worship.

But his plan of remaining in Homer was suddenly interrupted from an unexpected quarter.

Among my pupils while in Binghamton were two sons of Dr. R——, Silver Lake, Pa. These sons, who were boarders in my family, one of them older and the other younger than John, had ever been regarded by him with deep interest. Mrs. R——, in consequence of the recent death of her husband, was left a widow; and she, together with the elder children of the family, felt deeply anxious for the welfare of the younger members, whom they were desirous of having educated at home.

Some time in the month of February previous, a letter had been received from Mrs. R——, through Mr. M——, proposing the plan for John to become the teacher of her sons, in her family, for the period of two years. After maturely considering the application, an answer was returned expressive of my satisfaction with the offer, but rather hesitating as to the propriety of accepting it—mainly in view of John's age, in comparison with that of her eldest; which would render it more suitable for him to be his companion than his teacher.

After John had gone to Homer, another letter was received to this effect: inasmuch as their first plan had failed, and their present teacher had consented to remain—that I would allow John to make their house his home, for at least one year, as a companion to the lads, "on exactly the same footing as though we had adopted him, and he were really one of us." This request was urged with strong motives, drawn from the good he would be likely to do by his example and influence, and also by the advantage he might receive from the instruction of their teacher, and from their library.

This letter from Silver Lake I sent to John, with a request that he would take the subject into consideration, and acquaint me with the result of his views. The following is a copy of his reply; in which the reader will be struck not only with the traits of Christian character which it developes, but also the clearness of his mind and the comprehensiveness of his plans:

"HOMER, May 23, 1843.

"DEAR PARENTS—With respect to Mrs. R——'s letter, although I cannot say I have decided, yet I think I see some landmarks to point out the path of duty.

"In the first place, I think I can truly say, if I know any thing of my own heart, I wish only to know what is duty. From my infancy have you consecrated me to the service of God; and I have often made the same unreserved consecration myself. And now I do not wish to shrink from any duty which He may call me to perform.

"As to the want of religious privileges, of

which mother speaks, it is true there are great temptations in such circumstances; but are they any greater at Silver Lake than at most of our missionary stations? Where is the place to do good, if not in the midst of wickedness? I feel that, God's grace assisting me, I might be very useful there; and that, not so much to the surrounding population, though a wide field lies open in that respect: but I see those boys, and I think what a great influence for good or for evil they are destined to exert; and it appears to me, that whoever succeeds in giving their minds a right direction will be a benefactor to his country. If Mr. L—— stays too, as is possible, I shall have an opportunity of proceeding with my studies, and may not lose much in that line.

"On the other hand, two points present themselves. If Mr. L—— leaves, and I should spend two years there, I probably should not be able to enter college more than a year in advance. Whether it would be advisable to put back my collegiate course a year, you can judge better than I. My health now is very good, and the prospect is favorable that study will not injure it. But if Mr. L—— remains, and is well qualified to assist me—an important consideration—I may advance nearly as fast as I would in college. In either case these two difficulties arise: I must enter college in advance, which is not a good plan, ordinarily; and I run some risk of becoming so entangled with the kindness of the family, the charms of the place, and a sense of the great moral destitution, that I might find it difficult to tear myself away. If I could bring myself to feel that duty required me to go, at the expense of my studies, or that my usefulness would be greater to take such a situation now, with no other prospect but of continuing in it, than to wait until I have finished my course of study, I should have no hesitation on this point. But this I cannot do.

"The whole question is one of probabilities, and seems to be narrowed down to this: Is it probable, that if God should spare my life twenty or thirty years, my usefulness on the whole would be greater, if I should go to Silver Lake, or remain here? It appears to me, whenever I recur to the subject, that the probabilities are in favor of my remaining; but yet, my judgment may be warped by the pleasant situation for study in which I am now placed. I find, whenever I sit down to examine the matter closely, the idea of those boys growing up in sin, and exerting an influence fatal to religion, constantly presenting itself to my mind, and leading me to doubt what is my duty. I wish, dear father, you would write me, advising me what to do, and giving your reasons.

"Your affectionate son,

"J. D. L."

The substance of this communication was sent to Silver Lake, and other letters from the family were received urging the plan. At length John decided to go for one year; and one of the reasons assigned in his letter is the following, which is as valid as it is brief: "I am desirous to be educated, not merely to go to college."

On the 17th of June, John returned home from the academy, having been absent only two months, and bringing with him a note from the highly respected teacher, of which the following is a copy:

"HOMER, June 17, 1843.

"REV. P—— L——:

"DEAR SIR—It affords me great pleasure to be able to bear unqualified testimony to the correct deportment of your son, while he has been a member of our school. He has been diligent in the improvement of his time; and has acquired the character of an excellent scholar, and the esteem and respect of his fellow-students and teachers. He has mentioned to me that it may not be perfectly convenient for him to return.

"As the anniversary of our academy occurs at the close of the present term, we are very desirous that all our scholars should remain until the close—particularly so, those to whom parts in the public exercises have been assigned. I would therefore respectfully ask that your son may return, if you can make it consistent with your arrangements.

"With sincere respect, I am truly yours,

"S. B. W."

In compliance with the request contained in the foregoing, John returned to Homer in time to take the part assigned him at the anniversary in July.

On that occasion he delivered the following oration "On the Formation of Character." Uttering forth as he was the emotions of his own heart, as well as the results of his own reflections, he was listened to with deep interest; especially by the students, and by all who knew him.

ORATION.

"To a youth about to enter upon the active scenes of life, his future employment is a subject of deep interest. And if intelligent and judicious, he will act upon this principle—that in choosing an occupation, he should select that which he is willing to make the permanent business of life.

"The principle is certainly a reasonable one; and it is susceptible of a far higher application than merely to the choice of a profession.

"Youth, too, is the period for the formation of the character; and that, not merely for time. In view of this fact, it is evident that an investigation into the nature and consequences of the characters between which we are called to choose, must be of the highest importance.

"If we enter upon such an investigation, we shall find four candidates, each eager for the throne of our hearts. And in making from them our selection, let us not forget our principle—to choose that which we mean always to retain, and which we are willing to follow, whenever and wherever it leads us.

"First comes AMBITION, ever striving for the first rank, and assuming as her motto, 'Rather reign in hell, than serve in heaven.' Her votary, setting before himself some point of honor or distinction far in futurity, pursues it solely for the power and distinction which it will bring to him. Go ask yonder artist, toiling night and day, and yet poor, if he would accept at your hands of the wealth of Crœsus, on condition of forsaking his employment, and giving up the hope of being ultimately numbered with Michael Angelo, Raphael, and our own illustrious West. Think you he would accept your offer? No. What cares he for wealth, if he must have it by the loss of his idol, fame? Had you offered to Alexander, Cæsar, or Napoleon, the wealth which they actually acquired, on condition of their engaging in commercial pursuits, think you they would not have spurned the offer with indignation? Their object was glory; and upon its attainment they were bent, though seas of blood should obstruct their progress.

"In this character we can discover many valuable traits. Such are, *the fixedness of purpose*, *the unconquerable perseverance*, *the nice sense of honor*, *and the never-failing spirit of hope*, which influence the truly ambitious man. But when we look at the other side, what a fearful picture presents itself: *supreme devotion to self*, *the entire disregard of others*, *and the determination to be first*, *let what will come*—traits which characterize every one actuated by no higher motive. Rivers of blood have flowed in the track of ambitious military men; and the tears and groans of the millions of the helpless and innocent, have cried for vengeance too long to make the path of military glory desirable. He who strives for the first rank among the literati, or the statesmen of our country, does not, necessarily, thus outrage the finer feelings of our nature. But he is perplexed with fear, lest he shall lose his present honors, or fail in his strife for those still higher, which like a deadly worm gnaws into his heart, producing sleepless nights and days of distracting anxiety. And should his worst fears be realized, where then is his resource? How many have been thrown back into obscurity, and recalling their too hasty choice of character, have turned their course in some more peaceful direction.

"But suppose the votary of ambition realizes his hopes, and attains the summit of earthly glory. When he has travelled this thorny path, until ambition herself can ask him to go no further, is he then at rest? Has that deadly worm lost its hold upon his heart? Still it rankles there, and may consume his very vitals. In the words of another, 'The road on which ambition travels has this disadvantage. The higher it ascends, the more difficult it becomes, until it terminates on some elevation too steep for safety, and too sharp for repose; and where the wretched occupant, above the sympathy of men, and below the friendship of angels, resembles in the solitude, if not in the depth of his misery, a Prometheus chained to the Causasian rock.'

"With a heavy heart we turn from this picture, and find our next candidate, PLEASURE, with a smiling countenance, engaging to dispel every cloud, and shouting in the ecstasy of her joy, 'A short life, and a merry one.' Her votaries are distinguished for *wit* and *humor*, a *noble generosity*, a *nice sense of honor, and a desire to cast off care*, and live in mirth and gayety. But here, as before, our business is with consequences. 'Consequences!' exclaims the nymph; 'of these my votaries think not.' 'However,' we reply, 'permit us, in our search after truth, carefully to lift the curtain from the death-bed scene of one who had been most unrestrained in his indulgence in sensual pleasure. But what have we here? Humanity, turn away and weep over the deep disgrace. Is this a man? Did he ever wear the image of the Deity? Is it possible that he was once the gayest of the gay, in the halls of fashion; that his wit was always the brightest, his laugh the merriest, and his song the best, of all the butterfly spirits who flitted in the sunbeams of present enjoyment? Aye, and the causes of his downfall may be found in those very things with which fortune would seem most highly to have favored him. He was flattered, courted, and admired by all his acquaintance. Vain of his acquirements, and intoxicated with the attention which he received, he dipped his wings a little deeper in the pursuit of pleasure; and at length, casting off one by one all the restraints which education or pride had imposed, he rushed madly on—every year drawn further into the fatal maelstrom, and at every whirl sinking deeper in vice and vicious amusements, until, his property, his health, and his reputation being entirely swallowed up, and his life almost gone, he cries out, anxious to repair some of the mischiefs of his past life, 'Oh, that every youth could see me, and take warning from me, to form no character which he is unwilling to follow in its consequences!'

"But as we leave this character in disgust, shall we cast ourselves into the golden stream, and sail with the multitudes who are in the pursuit of wealth, making riches their god, and following Avarice as their leader? Many indeed, escaping sensuality, rush to the other extreme, and seek by excessive parsimony to atone for excessive dissipation. But before submitting ourselves to her influence, what are her real claims to the throne of our hearts? Is not her ruling principle a supreme love of money? And to what crimes have men not been led by this same principle? The power of avarice, when it has full possession of a man, knows no bounds but death. Behold yonder rich, but wretched victim of this passion, mistaken for a beggar by a compassionate gentleman, and humbly receiving a penny at his hand. Follow him, as he proceeds from one base act to another, until—devoid of all sensibility, and with a heart so steeled, that he must have the pound of flesh containing the life's blood, as the forfeit of his bond—he throws a heap of straw into one corner of his mud floor, flings himself upon it, and while heaps of gold and silver are concealed in the holes and crevices of his miserable hovel, leaves the world, an object of universal pity and contempt.

"But where shall we go? Ambition, pleasure, and avarice, are each found unworthy of our confidence. And are we forced to the conclusion that whatever character we form, entire submission to it will render us miserable? One candidate yet remains. Where will RELIGION lead us? Her appearance is, at first view, forbidding. And although her promises are rich and numerous, yet the price of her favor is so humbling to the pride of the natural heart, that few comparatively can be induced to pay it. She will accept of nothing less than an entire and unconditional surrender of the whole soul to a principle of duty; allowing no motive of self-interest, love of ease, or desire of happiness to interfere with her claims. And, in return, she promises no exemption from the common calamities and reverses of life, no uninterrupted course of prosperity. And her only resource in adverse circumstances, is a consciousness of having acted from a sense of right. Honor, pleasure, and wealth, as the objects of life, she despises, and values them only as means of glorifying our Creator, and benefiting our fellow-creatures.

"The truly religious man, taking his stand on the broad principle of doing *right*, though the heavens should fall, and actuated by a burning desire growing out of that principle, to be of some use in the world, girds himself for a life of toil and hardship if need be, to accomplish this end. What cares he for the glittering dust, with which so many are dazzled? If it comes in his way, he takes it; and uses it to the glory of Him who gave it, and with thankfulness for the more extended good which he is thus enabled to do. And if it is taken from him, he resigns it without a murmur; only regretting that he had not used more of it in works of Christian charity. What cares he for the enticements of pleasure? He finds infinitely higher enjoyment in doing his Master's will, than do the votaries of pleasure in the ball-room, the theatre, the gambling-house, or the brothel.

"And think you he casts a wishful eye at the prospects which ambition holds out? He acts from a far higher motive. His feet are planted on an elevation, from which Napoleon's greatness is—nothing. If honor is presented to him, he receives it. And while he holds it, exerts all his energies to use it aright. And should he lose all his honors, he could give them up without a pang; for the gnawing restlessness of the ambitious man is a stranger to his breast.

"But for the full development of his character, he looks beyond this world. As we remarked in the outset, in forming a character, we are doing a work not merely for time, but for eternity. Viewed in this light, how do the distinctions of this world, as well as its pleasures and its wealth, fade away in the distance. Who is ready to carry a spirit of ambition into *eternity?* Who will hope to engage in the dance, the game of cards, or to find the intoxicating draught, in *eternity?* Or who can carry with him his bags of gold, his houses, or his lands, to feast his eyes upon them in a world of spirits?

"But the man whose character has been formed upon religion as its foundation, will there enjoy honors which transcend the power of language to describe. Angels and archangels shall be his companions; and with them he will be for ever rising to higher attainments. *Pleasure!* he will bathe in an ocean of it, without a bottom and without a shore. *Riches!* he will walk the golden streets of the celestial city. A mansion in heaven shall be his—a mansion which the wealth of millions of worlds would not purchase. Nothing will be wanting to perfect his happiness. And as he looks back after countless ages have rolled by upon his little span of existence on this earth, a feeling of unmingled joy will arise, that honor, pleasure, and wealth had none of them such charms for him as unassuming piety."

Among the papers dated "Homer," is the following, which appears to be a composition prepared as an exercise of the academy. It will now be read with interest, in view of the early departure of the writer, to test the truth of his theory.

"A DREAM.

"The day on which it was supposed by many that the world would come to an end, was a delightful Sabbath in the spring. It seemed more delightful from the fact that the winter had been a long and severe one, and spring was just appearing in all her loveliness. The grass upon the hills had just begun to look green; the daffodils and hyacinths in the garden were just peeping above the ground; and all nature had that cheerful aspect which, it would seem, ought to fill every heart with grateful praise to the Giver of every good and perfect gift.

"My mind, during the day, had been made solemn by thinking of the great expected event. For though I place no confidence in Mr. Miller's theory, yet it certainly cannot be right to ridicule a subject so solemn. My thoughts had dwelt a good deal upon the prophecies, and had become a good deal confused.

"In this state of mind, I sat down near the close of the day, reflecting on the impossibility of fixing a time for the appearance of the Son of man, when the word of God expressly says, 'Of that day and hour knoweth no man.' My train of thought was suddenly interrupted, and I became conscious that I was in the eternal world. But I saw no golden streets, or pearly gates, or precious stones sparkling on every side. I did not even see the great white throne, nor the many other things which we have been accustomed to associate with the name of heaven. Nor did I see the saints with crowns on their heads, and palms in their hands.

But I *felt* a sense of the presence of Deity, so strong as to be even painful. The very air was love. An idea far fainter than you would receive of the sun by looking at a glow-worm, may be obtained of the intense blaze of divine love, by recurring to a season when the influences of the Holy Spirit are filling a place, and scores are flying to the ark of safety. A stranger at such a time sees a chastened seriousness upon nearly every brow, and feels that he is in an atmosphere of holiness. I *felt* also the presence of the saints. I *felt* that I myself was disrobed of my body, and by means of the secret 'tie that binds our hearts in kindred love,' I perceived myself surrounded with thousands of saints and angels, and archangels; and *perceived*, for the sound was too ethereal to be heard, the rich strains of the heavenly harp, accompanied by the holy song of myriads of saints and angels in happy chorus.

"By means of the new power to communicate my ideas of which I found myself possessed, I asked one of the former why the situation of the finally happy was so different from all my preconceived opinions. To clothe the ideas which he advanced in reply with suitable words, would require an angel's pen. I can only give their substance as it appeared to me. 'You speak,' said he, 'of expecting to *see* pearly gates, golden streets, a river of life lined with the tree of life, and high above every thing the throne of God. So once did I, even till I burst the fetters which bound me to my vile body, and ascended to be for ever with my Saviour. In him I have found more than I could have asked or thought. There is no need here of the sun or of the moon; for the Lamb is our light. We more than realize all our conceptions of beauty and splendor; and in him we have our all in all. So, that although our spirits are invisible as air, and unaffected by objects which on earth influence the mind through the sense; yet, in the communion of one kindred heart with another, and of all with our great elder Brother, we find happiness, of which the glorious images and highly wrought comparisons of the Scriptures convey but a faint idea.'

"Encouraged by his kindness, I ventured to ask him still further, respecting the time of Christ's coming to judgment. 'Go,' exclaimed he, while I felt, by means of the mysterious influence which connected our souls, that the holy fire of love in his heart was burning with fresh ardor—'Go, correct the erroneous impressions that are so widely prevalent on this subject. And when you return to earth, I pray you, cease not to testify to the truth in this matter. Christ will come to judge the earth; 'but of that hour knoweth no man.' *We* know it not. The very wisest of the archangels desires to look into these things, but with cheerful resignation yields his desire to the will of Jehovah. How absurd, then, for puny mortals to attempt to pry into the counsels of the Most High.

"'But Christ is coming for judgment, not merely at the end of the world. He comes often, and often when he is not expected. Whenever the bell tolls the knell of death, he has come. Whenever the coffin is borne through the streets, he has come. When the infant is taken by the hand of death, when blooming youth is snatched away, when manhood withers and falls, when old age drops into the grave, when one is crushed by a falling tree or struck dead by lightning, in all these cases Christ has come to judgment. Go, then, and apply this truth to the hearts of men. And endeavor to make them feel, that as individuals they should be prepared for the coming of the day of the Lord.'

"I awoke, for I had been dreaming. And yet I felt that it was not all a dream. The clearness with which I had been enabled to perceive the uncertainty of the time when Christ would come to every one by death, and yet the certainty that he would thus come, had tranquillized my mind. And as I gazed upon the lovely face of nature around me, and the glorious sun just setting in a blaze of beauty, my heart rose in gratitude 'to my Father who made it all;' and I vowed to spend my life in leading men to the Lamb of God, that they may be prepared for his coming at the GREAT LAST DAY."

Among other papers of this date, is an interesting review of Stephens' "Central America," which shows that during his residence in Homer he had read that work with attention.

Also a small memorandum-book, written in

pencil, and labelled "Stray Thoughts, No. 1," filled with short articles like the following:

"INFLUENCES OF GOD'S SPIRIT IN SUBDUING HEARTS.—Did you ever see the eaves of a house fringed with icicles, and the pleasant sun of a spring morning pouring his beams upon them? How they fall, one after another, melted by his genial influences. Even the largest and strongest, that which has been growing all winter, is at length obliged to yield, and falls to the ground broken in a thousand pieces. And then did you look at the same roof after the heat of the day, and see that not one of those mementos of winter remains—that all are made trophies of the warming and softening influences of the glorious sun? Even so, when the Sun of righteousness arises upon a congregation of hardened sinners, by the influences of his Spirit, one by one they are brought to the foot of the cross, subdued by the power of Jesus' love. Even those who have grown old in the service of Satan, and whose hearts are as hard as the nether millstone, are unable to resist his gentle call, appealing to every generous thought and grateful feeling, until in some instances hardly an individual in the community is left impenitent."

"How tender was the affection which Jesus possessed for the family at Bethany! And how happy is that family where all are beloved by Jesus! Who can read the account of the resurrection of Lazarus without tears? 'Jesus wept.' How well is *he* fitted for our Mediator, who could thus sympathize with sorrow while here on earth."

"A Thought for Self-examination.—In confessing sin I always feel as though, even if God could forgive me, I never could forgive myself."

"The Reckoning Time.—'After a long time, the lord of those servants cometh and reckoneth with them.' How does the disobedient son of an affectionate, yet strict father feel, when, after a day of uncommon rebellion, he hears, 'My son, I must have a reckoning with you.' How does the fraudulent clerk grow pale with terror, when his employer announces his determination to have a reckoning with those to whom he has committed his business. What horrors gather upon the criminal, when the day of reckoning comes with the violated human law; and what infinitely greater horrors will torment the one who has violated God's moral law, when the last great day of reckoning shall come!"

"'Then Paul and Barnabas waxed bold.' They waxed—not angry, not impatient with the Jews—but *bold.* Their message had as much of love, and was quite as free to the Jews as before."

## CHAPTER VI.

### RESIDENCE AT SILVER LAKE.

The last week in July, John went to Silver Lake. This is the name of a town in Susquehannah county, Penn., about eight miles north of Montrose, and about twelve south from Binghamton.

Some twenty or thirty years ago, one hundred and ten thousand acres of land in that part of the state were purchased by Dr. R—— of Philadelphia, who with his wife came to reside within the limits of the purchase, while the country for miles around was an unbroken wilderness. On the shore of a beautiful sheet of water, which the enterprising owner called Silver Lake, a tasteful mansion was erected, and the adjacent ground laid out in imitation of European scenery. A description of the doctor's tract of land was drawn up by an English gentleman, and sent across the Atlantic; in consequence of which a number of foreigners came over to settle on the tract. An unusual proportion of the inhabitants at the present time are Irish Roman-catholics. And one object which John hoped to accomplish in his new situation, was to benefit these by furnishing them with religious reading, especially with the Holy Bible.

In the bosom of this retired, wealthy, and honorable family, John remained till the middle of the following April; when, owing to an unexpected arrangement, by which the family at the Lake was to be absent for some months, he returned to his parents in Berkshire.

Secluded in an uncommon degree from intercourse with the surrounding population, this family had become accustomed to look for sources of enjoyment within themselves. During the long winter evenings they were together, John being one of them; when the time was agreeably filled up with conversation or with reading. And the library which Doctor R—— had collected being for its extent and variety perhaps unequalled in this country as a private gentleman's library, there was no danger of exhausting that source of profit and amusement. By intercourse with the elder members of this family, and the intelligent friends that visited them, John's colloquial powers were perceptibly developed. Always interesting and instructive in the social circle, he afterwards become still more so.

The welfare of his young associates, for whose benefit especially he had been invited to become a member of the family, he never for a moment seemed to lose sight of. To aid them in their studies, and to improve their moral character, was his constant aim and the subject of his daily prayers.

In connection with the teacher and one or two other pious individuals, he aided in sustaining a Sabbath-school and a weekly prayer-meeting, in a private house several miles distant from the Lake. In the same place there was preaching by a missionary once in two weeks. And on the Sabbath, when there was no preaching, a congregation regularly assembled to hear a sermon read, and the other exercises of public worship performed, by these same individuals. From the depositories in Binghamton he procured religious tracts, which he distributed as he had opportunity, and Bibles and Testaments, with which he supplied several families.

Since writing the above, I have received from Mr. and Mrs. Simpson, intelligent as well as devoted and experienced Christians of the Scotch school, residing on the premises, a communication; from which, as affording not only confirmation of the facts already stated, but evidence of the general estimation in which John was held in that vicinity, I take the liberty of copying the following extracts:

"SILVER LAKE, 19th July, 1845.

"MR. LOCKWOOD:

"DEAR SIR—Your dear son was a general favorite. Even the most regardless had to esteem him; and the most thoughtless were led to *think*, by the example that was before them. In his life and conversation, he was indeed a living epistle, seen and read of all men.

"Soon after your son came to Silver Lake, I found him not only pious and devoted to his Saviour, but also possessed of a great deal of that Christian charity that is not easily provoked.

"He became a teacher in the Sabbath-school

very soon after he came here; and was often requested to open the meeting with prayer; which he did with fervency, and in an impressive manner. His class were young girls, and some of them nearly his own age. And yet he seemed to feel himself as a father among them. And many times have I listened with pleasure to the affectionate manner in which he addressed them, and the apt illustrations that he used to explain and enforce the lessons they had been considering.

"He also took a willing part in our weekly prayer-meetings. His heart was engaged in them. And I have felt my mind stimulated to duty, and my heart refreshed, when joining with him in these exercises.

"He also attended the bed of sickness. There was one family in particular, where the mother had died; and the eldest son, who had attended her in her sickness, was dangerously ill. Your son went often to see him in company with a friend; and while they attended to his bodily wants, they directed the mind of the sufferer to the need he had of a Saviour; and their endeavors seemed to be blessed. The young man got better; and he told me that he felt as the psalmist had done, that it was good for him that he had known affliction.

"He seemed to be *always* awake to his duty, and anxious for the welfare of all. He sometimes called on our Catholic neighbors, and conversed with them on divine things, and distributed to all he found—who required and would receive them—Testaments and tracts. He used to loan his religious papers, that a greater number might read them; and gave away tracts to children and others. Indeed, he was a proof of how much good may be done with even slender means, when the heart and mind are engaged in the work.

"In the exercises of the family, he was often requested to lead in prayer; which he did with propriety of manner and expression. And I have been delighted with the ready way that he improved any opportunity of making his addresses to a throne of grace more impressive to those who joined with him in the exercise."

Mrs. Simpson adds, "All who have had the privilege of knowing the power of divine grace in the life and conversation of a humble Christian, could bear testimony how brightly it shone out in our departed friend, so early called to his reward. To all experienced with the waywardness of the youthful mind when not under that heavenly influence, it was really refreshing to see the effects upon him, in restraining and conquering every earthly feeling.

"His mild, gentle, and affectionate address and replies to all, gained even the esteem of those who were inclined to scoff at what they termed the over-strictness of the young instructor. He joined with cheerfulness in the innocent amusements of the young; and his example had an influence that was beneficial, to show the young that religion does not prevent any rational pleasure.

"A wish to do good seemed to be the ruling passion of his life. I have heard the mother of a family who lived in the woods say, that one dark, rainy night, when a feeling of loneliness had come over her, she was surprised to hear footsteps approaching; and her surprise was increased when Mr. Lockwood stepped in, with his cheerful voice and mild countenance, to try and lead them in the paths of peace. And he lent them from time to time books and papers, that he thought would be useful to them. And she said the friendly visits were oft repeated, and anxiously looked for by all the family.

"Yours with respect,

"J. SIMPSON."

Months after his death, I found among a mass of other papers of his stowed away in a box in the garret, a journal kept during his residence at the Lake, to the very existence of which I had till then been a stranger; which, though from its local and personal character it would be improper to submit it to the public eye, contains abundant and precious confirmation of the facts alluded to by Mr. and Mrs. Simpson; particularly of his self-denial in doing good, and of that charity which "is not easily provoked." The journal makes one hundred and ten pages quarto, foolscap, and is neatly written. A few extracts from it, on points connected with his religious exercises, are submitted as a specimen.

"SUNDAY, Oct. 1. Another Sabbath, in another month; was glad to have another opportunity of uniting with the people of God, in commemorating the dying love of Christ. It is also the communion-season in Berkshire; and I love to think that I have been remembered by my dear parents at the table of the Lord. They have been truly remembered by their absent son.

"SUNDAY, Dec. 31. The last time I shall write 1843. How swiftly it has passed. As I lay awake this morning, I took a review of the different circumstances in which I have been placed during the year. The state of trial and difficulty in which I spent my days, through last winter. The delightful occupations of my evenings, particularly when God's Spirit was poured out in Berkshire, and souls were turning to Christ. Father's installation. My two months in Homer, with all their pleasures and their pains. My return home. Visit of our New York friends, and the fact communicated by himself, of cousin W——'s new birth. Exhibition at Homer, and my residence here. What a note of praise should I render, that God has preserved me from my disease another year! If a year ago I could sing,

'Here, Lord, I give myself away,'

what should be my feelings *now?* Oh, Lord, I can do nothing more, even *now*, though my debt has increased so much. Take me, and make me as thou wouldst have me to be. If it please thee to spare me another year, may it be one of usefulness. And if not, may I be found in the path of duty, and prepared for the *welcome messenger;* for such may death be to me.

"SATURDAY, January 6. To-morrow is communion-season. I suppose it is also communion-season in Berkshire. How pleasant it will be to know that my parents are remembering me at the table of the Lord, at the same time when I am joining in the same delightful exercise. May I be enabled to examine myself thoroughly; to banish every worldly thought, and to receive new strength for future growth in grace.

"SABBATH, Jan. 7. Went to Friendsville. It has been to me a very interesting day: found it sweet to bring my friends in prayer to God. Felt particularly a burning desire that God would pour out his Spirit through all the surrounding country; prayed earnestly for the conversion of E——, who was present. My own dear brother had not a small share in my petitions; nor did I forget my dear parents, who perhaps were at the same time remembering me."

From the sequel it will appear that this "dear brother" had only a few days before been led, though unknown to John, to indulge hope in Christ.

"SUNDAY, Feb. 11. There has been a great deal of laughing, and light conversation in the family to-day. I should think all, and particularly those who profess to appreciate the Sabbath, would have no wish thus to desecrate its sacred hours. And yet I have laughed as much, and talked as lightly, as any one. But I trust I have repented of it: and if God spares my life till another Sabbath, I trust I shall be able to prove my repentance to be genuine. But perhaps I have already inflicted an injury on Christ's cause which I cannot repair. How do I know but some impenitent member of the family has been noticing my inconsistency? Perhaps Miss E——, and she will leave this week; so that I shall have no opportunity to efface the impression from her mind. Why did I not show that I really regarded the Sabbath's holy hours? 'The heart is deceitful above *all* things, and desperately wicked. Who can know it?' 'Search me, O God, and know my *heart;* try me, and know my *thoughts;* and see if there be any wicked way in me, and lead me in the way everlasting.'

"MONDAY, Feb. 12. Let fall this evening a remark about our conduct yesterday. I have reason to believe it was well received."

During the week he wrote the following to his friend in Cortland, for whom he had selected the texts of Scripture bearing on the duty of personal effort for the conversion of souls:

"SILVER LAKE, Feb. 16, 1843.

"DEAR WILLIAM—Your letter contained news of much interest to me, though a good deal of it of painful interest. Your own disappointment and sickness, and the situation of poor F—— had truly a *painful interest.* While the news that S. B—— was preparing for college, though it brought some anxiety for him, yet was *good news.* I was glad to hear that you still keep the temperance ball 'a rolling,' and to see the list of your officers for the missionary society, which shows you are awake on that subject.

"I wish you could look in upon me in my retreat. My health is good, and I am making progress, slow but sure, in my studies. A large library opens its rich treasures to me; a thing, by the way, often very injurious to a student, by inducing him to spend that time in reading which he ought to employ in exercise. To 'unbend the bow,' however, I walk a good deal, exercise myself in gymnastics, go out hunting with the boys, and when I can, turn a hand to the work on the farm. The family is a very pleasant one; and the evening circle is an infallible remedy for all the 'blues' one may have had through the day. Then, rarely a fortnight passes but brings some extra excitement, which takes me from my studies for a day, or half a day, and keeps me from becoming a mere book-worm. I hope, if I am spared, to enter Yale College next fall, freshman class; which I think I can do, with no trouble at all.

You see I don't mean to hurry myself. A life is before me, which it is not likely will be shortened by moderation: and if I am not through till my thirtieth birthday, why that is earlier than many useful men have become ministers.

"After all, is not this one great secret of the ill health among students, that they hurry too fast? In climbing the hill of science, those who expend all their thoughts upon the first steep pitch, must expect to be obliged to give out. The case is very often this—perhaps it may have been so with you: a young man comes from active business at a time of life when those who have always been studying are in college, and commences the preparatory course. He sees those of his own age so far ahead of him that his ambition is excited. He lays out for himself more than he ought to attempt, and more than he can accomplish; and then tries even to exceed that measure. His constitution, naturally good, sustains for a time the giddy whirl of the monotonous round, which is almost unbroken by exercise or any amusement; and he is thus led to believe he is not injured by it. He is *intoxicated*, as it were, with a passion for acquiring knowledge. And this passion, if indulged to excess, is almost as fatal to *health*, though of course not to *morality*, as a sensual passion. Thus our student, though he may perhaps live through college, is fairly 'used up' when he has hardly started in the race for knowledge. I rather wonder that students are not all *crazy*, than that so many are sick. I said, perhaps the picture may suit you. In its outlines I think it will. These accord with my own experience. It was this *student's intoxication* which took me from my studies at the age of twelve years, after having undermined a first-rate constitution; and then kept me for more than four years so that I did not feel safe from disease a day at a time. And I have reason to praise God that disease seized me so early in life, rather than at a later period. For now, by care, my constitution has been in a great degree restored, and I have learned to prize the gift of health too much to treat it lightly.

"You and I, dear William, have been in situations somewhat alike with regard to health, and we can sympathize with each other. I know

I am as liable to be sick as any body; and when sick, it is as hard for me as for any body to resign myself to God's will. But I'll tell you where I believe one difficulty lies in such cases. You remember, in Pilgrim's Progress, that when Christian came to the cross, his burden rolled off his shoulders, *and he saw it no more.* Now the trouble with *us* is, that even though we cast off our burden, we do not let it stay in the pit at the foot of the cross. Perhaps we go on singing a while, as he did; but our burden *will* come back. Now, if we could always feel, as it were, *careless* about ourselves, knowing that we have no temporal things to *care*, or fret ourselves for, we should get along much better.

"Do you often see Drs. Goodyear and Hyde? Their conversation has always been better than medicine, when I have been dejected. I suppose they tell you to have nothing to do with books, until your health is thoroughly established; and then to lay it down as a rule, 'Don't hurry. Study no more than you can easily bear. And when your health begins *in the least* to suffer, drop your books at once until you are well.' Why, even if the state of your lungs should forbid your ever hoping to blow 'the silver trumpet,' you have a respectable, profitable, and useful business upon which you can fall back; and thus you have 'two strings to your bow.' Write as soon as convenient, and believe me,

"Your affectionate brother in Christ,

"J. D. L."

The insertion of the preceding, though long, it is believed will be excused, inasmuch as it illustrates so clearly John's characteristic maturity of mind, comprehensive views of education, and heartfelt interest in others—and particularly in those placed by Providence in the trying situation of his beloved correspondent.

To proceed with extracts from the journal:

"SUNDAY, Feb. 18. Mr. S—— gave notice of a prayer-meeting next Wednesday evening. This is what I have long wished. I hope now to have a *weekly* opportunity of turning away from the world, and enjoying a season of social prayer. And my humble prayer is, also, that the season may not be without a blessing to the neighborhood where we go.

"SUNDAY, March 3. Had a very pleasant time in singing, after the evening service. 'Loving-kindness' was sung. What a sweet hymn to the believer:

> 'I'll with my last expiring breath,
> His *loving-kindness* sing—in death.'"

"TUESDAY, March 5. Three years ago to-day, was I last attacked by that disease which at one time caused my future prospects to look so gloomy. I well remember how depressed I was at the time, feeling that I should never be well. But God in his mercy has ordered it, that that dark time should close my night of affliction; and since then I have been constantly improving in health. How should I praise my heavenly Father, for all his mercies to me!"

"TUESDAY, March 13. Read in the family this evening in 'Home.' Am sorry to see Miss Bremer display Socinianism so decidedly. The description of a death-bed scene came in this evening, and the name of Christ was not once mentioned; and he was only once alluded to, thus: that '*one of our own number* had been into another world, and returned thence with the same human nature; thus offering us light on the dark journey.' How blessed it is to feel '*none but Christ;*' and what a hollow pretension of religion is found in any belief which does not make him all in all."

"THURSDAY, March 14. I like my *moss hunting*. And as I have such a good opportunity here of analyzing plants, I think I shall devote my afternoons exclusively to botany. How sweet is it, particularly to the Christian, to engage in the study of any of the natural sciences; to see the evident marks of design, and nice adaptation of the means to the end, in the most insignificant of the mosses. And how still more delightful to feel, 'my Father made them all,' and can he be unmindful of me?"

"SATURDAY, March 16. Went this afternoon on a tour which I had been long contemplating, to distribute tracts. The rain was pouring down all the afternoon, and the road was exceedingly muddy, but I had a very pleasant time."

"THURSDAY, March 28. Went over to see C——. How much I find my spirits freshened, and my soul revived by these visits.

C—— is now able to be up most of the time. He still appears well; has commenced family prayer, and manifests a determination to live for God. God grant that he may hold out."

About this time he wrote as follows, to an acquaintance in the Theological Institution, Hamilton, N. Y.:

"DEAR L—— —A fine field for usefulness is open in this region. O that I had the time, the zeal, and the ability to occupy it! I put forth a few feeble efforts; but what is that? L——, we must work while the day lasts; for the night cometh, when no man can work. Many opportunities, which we are apt to think of little importance, are daily afforded us, of doing good to the cause of Christ. As a student, even, and for the sake of refreshing my spirits, I often find a religious conversation, after a walk to some of the neighbors' houses, do me more good than any thing else. . . . . Does R—— continue firm for the ministry? He should not kill himself then with study. Write at your earliest convenience; and believe me

"Your true friend and Christian brother,

"J. D. L."

I add only the following short extracts from the journal:

"MONDAY, April 1. Mr. —— has proposed to me to write a lecture, to deliver at Friendsville next week in his stead, as he will not have time to fulfil his engagement: should like to do it, and perhaps I may. Gathered this afternoon, for Miss C——, some of 'Cenomyce rangiferina,' or reindeer's lichen."

"THURSDAY, April 4. Have been driving on my botanical lecture."

'SUNDAY, April 7. Communion-day, as I suppose, in Berkshire. I know my dear parents remember me, as also I know I have remembered them."

"TUESDAY, April 9. Went over to Friendsville this evening, and delivered my lecture."

The last entry reads thus:

"THURSDAY, April 11. Went to —— this evening. Spoke to the people of my parting. Some were affected to tears. After meeting, endeavored to impress on some of the young men the necessity of a change of heart; but it seemed to do no good. Oh, Lord, arise and breathe upon these slain, that they may live. Thy Spirit alone can reach their hard hearts."

Among the papers of this date I find, written with a lead-pencil, a manuscript volume of one hundred and fourteen pages, entitled, "Notes on Hume's England." It gives a condensed view of the contents of each chapter, with the page on which each item noted may be found. The notes are brought down to the fifth volume, A. D. 1643. From this, it appears that he not only read, but read attentively that celebrated work during this period.

Other papers show that he devoted some attention at this time to the science of chemistry. Being favorably situated for the study of botany, he indulged himself with increasing his knowledge of that science. And the lecture to which allusion is made in the journal, is proof of his success in that study. From comparing dates, it will be seen that only eight days intervened, and one of them was of course the Sabbath, from the time Mr. —— made the request to him to take his place, and the evening of its delivery. And an inspection of the journal shows that it must have been the work of only a few of those remaining days. Though evidently only the first draft of his pen, and bearing marks of being drawn up in haste, extracts from it are inserted, not only with a view of presenting a more complete portrait of the writer, showing his object and his spirit, but with the hope that some of the sentiments expressed may be of advantage to the youthful reader. The lecture opens with the following introduction:

"Thomas Jefferson, after giving a graphic description of that great curiosity, the Natural Bridge in Virginia, remarks that hundreds who have always lived within twenty miles of the place have never seen it. We wonder at the insensibility of these people to the beautiful and the grand in nature; while, at the very moment, we are living in perhaps still greater insensibility to a thousand beauties scattered within twenty *rods* of our own doors, by the same hand which spanned that stupendous arch."

Then follows a history of the science of botany; ending with a brief review of the Linnæan, or artificial system. This part of the manuscript evinces an intimate acquaintance with the subject. Omitting it, however, as being of interest only to a scientific botanist, the following at the conclusion is presented, as suited to attract attention among youthful readers generally. After bringing before the mind the different seasons of the year, with the flowers peculiar to each, and showing that botany can be studied at any season of the year, it is added, "The botanist, when he has once analyzed a flower, will ever after hail with delight its first appearance, as that of an old acquaintance. If we would make our acquaintances of this kind more numerous, how seldom should we have cause to complain of neglect and coldness on the part of those whom we thought our friends.

"In the world, the best rule is, 'Make few intimate friends;' but the botanist need not be thus fettered. *He* may make his dear, though silent friends as numerous as he pleases; and as their number increases, he will be able to view them with more and yet more satisfaction, as they look smilingly to heaven from their humble bed, teaching *him* also to acknowledge with gratitude the source whence flow his numerous blessings; or bend their lofty heads in graceful humility, instructing *him* by their example to be 'meek and lowly of heart.' And when adversity howls about him, and, of his human friends, some have faithlessly deserted him, and others are unable *themselves* to breast the storm, much less to sustain *him*, he perchance may find in one of his botanical rambles, which will now become doubly dear, a clematis which has attached itself to a fragile trellis, and along with its impotent supporter been hurled to the ground by the hurricane of the night before; while its neighbor, having fortunately clung to an oak strengthened by the storm of centuries, remains unharmed: the sight will recall to his mind the exclamation of David, 'It is better to trust in the Lord, than to put confidence in princes;' and he will return home, firmly resolved to seek no other support than the arm of the mighty God of Jacob.

"I am young; and, I trust, may be permitted to encourage attention to botany in my friends who are also young. I am fond, at the proper time, of amusement, of recreation; and I trust

I may be permitted to recommend to those who are also fond of amusement, a pursuit fitter for that name than any of the vain, frivolous, destructive, and often vicious sports in which youth so often engage. Are you fond of light conversation and gay company? Assemble a group, and sally forth in quest of flowers. You will neither want disposition to talk, nor subjects to talk upon.

"Are you enamoured of the dance, and enlivened by the vivacity of the ballroom? Go into the fields, with the grass for your carpet, the birds for your music, and the flowers for your party, and your heart will bound within you. You will feel inclined to dance, rather than walk; and this inclination will be the natural overflowing of a joyful heart, not the unnatural excitement of champagne and the fiddle. And when you return from your ramble, you will not have an aching head and a system unfit for business; but every power will be invigorated. Your pulse will beat freer; and you will wish for another leisure hour, to renew your innocent sport.

"Are you fond of hunting or fishing? Of

course, then, you are accustomed to ramble in the woods, and by the side of streams—exactly the places for flowers. And if you are so eager in the search for game, whose wanton death is to the humane mind so distressing; how much more eager will you not be to pursue the game of the naturalist, to obtain which you need no destruction of life. If you sometimes hunt for days together with no success, and still are as fond of the chase as ever, you would have *this* advantage in becoming a botanist: you would never be disappointed in obtaining your game. You can hardly walk half a mile without finding some new curiosity. And the variety which you find, and the necessity of looking sometimes closely, keep up the interest of the excursion, and prevent it from becoming a dull monotony.

"But are you fond—I hope for the honor of your village none can answer in the affirmative—are you fond of the intoxicating draught? If you have become a slave to liquor, I must take it for granted, that in this day of temperance you wish to be freed from its baneful influence. If indeed you do, try botany for your cure. Whenever your *un*natural thirst seizes you, fly to the fields in search of flowers, instead of the tavern in search of liquid fire. Raise your spirits *naturally* by the exhilarating influence of the fresh air, and the delight of adding a new specimen to your collection; and not artificially and *unnaturally*, by the glass which poisons while it excites.

"Are you a utilitarian, a matter-of-fact person? And do you undertake nothing which does not promise to be of real, tangible use? Here, again, you may be suited with botany. If you believe that knowledge is useful, and that our minds are strengthened by exercise, you will cultivate this science to improve your memory, as you do the mathematics for your reasoning powers, or the languages to acquire fluency of speech. If your memory is defective, you will scarcely find any thing better designed to strengthen it.

"Another advantage in this science is, the love of order which it induces. You will find every plant occupying a particular place in the great system; and whatever be the minor differences of height, color, and sometimes of shape, you will always find it in that place. The very act of analysis requires classification. And if you make an herbarium, a thing which a botanist seldom neglects, you will find a good exercise of your taste in its arrangement. You may often be placed in situations where it is of the utmost importance to know whether a plant is nutritious or poisonous. Will it not then be useful to know that any plant whose flower has more than twelve stamens all inserted on the calyx, may be eaten with impunity; that one which has but five stamens, one pistil, and a berry-like seed, is poisonous, wherever it be found? These facts, and others of the same nature, botany teaches. It also speaks of the medicinal qualities of plants; and tells with certainty, not only the properties which are possessed in common by whole tribes, but also what particular species possesses those properties in greatest abundance. Thus you will discover that the poppy and the bloodroot are alike narcotic or stupefying; and also what kind of poppy is so highly narcotic as to be profitable in the manufacture of opium.

"Lastly, are you a Christian? And do you take more than ordinary delight in looking upon the works of nature—feeling that you can 'look from nature up to nature's God?' Are you rejoiced when you see the evident tokens of design running through all the works of our Creator; and do you view each new instance of nice adaptation as a new proof that 'my Father made them all?' Where can you more fitly indulge these feelings than during a botanical walk? You see, in the spring, the delicate bud which has been preserved by a scaly coat from winter's cold, gradually expanding; and at length, when the continued warmth convinces it that it is time to make its appearance, bursting the shell as if by instinct, and springing out a verdant leaf or a fragrant flower. You see again, in autumn, another embryo surrounded by another covering, to resist the frosts of another winter, while all the old leaves are stripped off, to prevent the snow from crushing the branches to the ground. The evergreens, indeed, retain their foliage; but in relation to *them*, you see that their needle-shaped leaves are better adapted than any others could be, to prevent a burden of snow from accumulating upon them. These are but common examples of the wonderful proofs of a plan in the creation. On every side you find them. Even the gaudy colors of many flowers, if they have no other design, may serve to teach us, 'If God so clothe the grass of the field, which to-day is, and to-morrow is cast into the oven, how much more will he clothe you?'

"Your delight in your rambles will be greatly increased by this last reflection. All nature will seem to rejoice, and will call upon you to join in its song of gratitude to the Giver of every good and perfect gift. You will find it happiness enough to *live*, without resorting to any artificial means to increase that happiness. And you will constantly derive more and more pleasure from the hours you devote to *the science of botany*."

During the period of his residence at the Lake, John reviewed his classical studies, with a view of offering himself, the next fall, as a candidate for the Freshman class in Yale College.

He wrote to his parents regularly, once in three weeks; and those letters are specimens of filial and fraternal love. While it is not to be supposed that a stranger will feel an interest in the perusal of such letters, in mass, even if it were right to publish them, it is thought that those who have followed the departed one thus far, would like to see a few extracts *from these*, which go still further to illustrate his character as an intelligent and devoted Christian.

Under date of February 26, he thus writes: "Had a long and friendly discussion with Miss E. W——," an accomplished lady, intimate at Silver Lake, and teaching the Catholic Female Seminary in B——. "Miss E—— does not believe in the infallibility of the pope—says that very few Catholics do; only prays to the saints as one Christian friend on earth would ask another to pray for him; and considers it as an unspeakable source of consolation that she *hopes to go to purgatory*. She concluded by offering to pray to the saints to pray for *me*. I told her that if she would direct her supplications directly to Christ, I would reciprocate the favor. She said she would. I do indeed pray for her. I assure you it quickens my spirit of devotion, when I see such excellent people so strict and devout in their attendance upon the cold forms and useless and idolatrous rites of the most perfect system of delusion that the enemy of God and man has ever invented."

In allusion to some pleasing and unexpected occurrences in connection with our family, of which I had apprized him, he writes, "How often is it, that such pleasant coincidences as that of which you speak happen in our family. Or is it because we 'eye' Providence more closely than some others?"

Perhaps this is as proper a place as anywhere in the volume to present a testimony to the character of John, coming from an unexpected quarter. The following is to Mrs. Lockwood, from our friend Mrs. W——, mother to Miss E——, and shows that, notwithstanding his views respecting Romanism were as already expressed in the last letter, his character and conduct were such as to command the respect and win the affection of intelligent Romanists, instead of prejudicing them against him:

"My dear Mrs. Lockwood—I cannot let dear M——'s letter go, without expressing my deep sympathy in your sad bereavement. It must be a gratification, though a melancholy one, that your excellent son was admired by all who knew him; and that his meek and pious character carries with it a conviction of his present happiness. He was one of those, my dear Mrs. Lockwood, whom *our* church reckons among her members, though separated; as I feel assured he loved God sincerely, and would therefore sacrifice all for the truth, if he only knew where to find it. May God in his mercy console you and your dear husband, and strengthen you both to submit to his will without repining.

"Truly and sincerely yours, etc.,

"B. W."

In the last letter received from him at Silver Lake, and dated March 22, 1844, he thus writes in view of his future course: "I should like, if possible, to be in some situation where I could pay my way, or at least partly do it. I could teach any thing that would commonly be required in a school in the country, except the higher mathematics. I think I could teach botany, if it were necessary. I want to pay some attention to that this summer. I am now so far advanced in the languages, that I need not hurry. And botany, besides, would give me as much exercise as I would need.

"To give you a view of my state of preparation, I shall finish, next week, the fifth book of Xenophon; and at the rate I am now going on, it will take me a month to get the other two. This I hope to accomplish, and then read a little in the poetry of the Greek Reader. I have read the Æneid of Virgil, the Jugurtha of Sallust, and nearly half of Cicero. Latin comes so easy to me, that I shall be able to finish the remainder of each of these without much difficulty. Writing Latin, which they require at Yale, is very easily learnt. I ought to look over my arithmetic, if I could, in some of its higher applications. And this is another reason why I should like to assist some teacher. I might review my arithmetic while teaching it.

"I can think of no school I should like so well as Mr. Marsh's. Perhaps he may want my assistance. But if not, I can take up with him any book I choose. In any he is well qualified to assist me. I shall have a good opportunity to pursue my botany and music also. And then, above all, I could see dear home once a fortnight—coming up Friday evening, so as to attend the singing-school.

"And now, dear father, though it is looking a good ways ahead, I will propose an arrangement for my college life. You know —— is very anxious to go to college, but his father can hardly afford it. Can I not *hire and furnish a room*, and then invite him to share it with me? This would somewhat lessen his expenses. And with this arrangement perhaps his father would feel able to send him. I would rather you would say nothing about it to his family until you make some decision. I think —— would be as good a room-mate as I could have, and I might be useful to him."

## CHAPTER VII.

### RESIDENCE IN BERKSHIRE AGAIN.

On the 15th of April, 1844, John arrived in Berkshire, in good health and spirits; and in every respect greatly benefited by his rustication at the Lake, and on the hills of Susquehannah county.

Instead of adopting the course suggested by him in his last, it was determined, that as the rest of the family wished to visit the city of New York in the month of May, he, together with the hired girl, should remain and keep the house open; and then, and afterwards—as it would be a broken term—pursue his studies until August, at home, in the same way as he had done at Silver Lake. To this arrangement the dear child submitted, though it evidently cost him a severe struggle.

As soon as the season permitted, he began to cultivate the garden, and the flower-bed in front of the house; engaging in any thing within his power which he saw necessary to be done, or conducive to our comfort, with his accustomed alacrity.

After the departure of the family for the city, on the first week in May, he, with his characteristic love of order, distributed his time; endeavoring to apportion it judiciously between study, exercise, devotion, etc. At this time, having been preserved from his fits for more than three years, neither he nor his friends apprehended much danger of their recurrence. In this, however, we were all destined to be disappointed. He was seized again, between 11 and 12 o'clock on the night of Saturday, the 25th of May, and under circumstances peculiarly afflicting.

On that evening, and not an hour previous, I had arrived from New York, accompanied by a young Christian brother from Cortland, an intimate friend of John's. Occupying a room on the first floor, he was awakened by my knocking at his bedroom window; and on recognizing my voice, arose and admitted us into the house.

Delighted of course to see us, he proposed to get for us some refreshment without awaking the hired girl. He did so; and while we were partaking of it, became very much engaged in telling me of an occurrence which, during my absence, had taken place within the bounds of the congregation. He, in connection with several others who were engaged in conducting a stated prayer-meeting, had been arraigned before a justice court; he however being only summoned as a witness. The occurrence was a disgraceful one on the part of the prosecutors, exciting the whole of the religious part of the community, and enlisting their sympathies in favor of the defendants; but the particulars it would be occupying too much space to give in this small volume. Suffice it to say, it was an occurrence of absorbing interest in the neighborhood, and one which for the fortnight previous had severely taxed John's nervous system.

While thus engaged in apprizing me of the history of this transaction, he became convulsed. The fit was light, however, compared with those of former years. This being the first of his attacks since we lived in Berkshire, it was thought advisable to say nothing about it, except to the family physician. On the

Sabbath he attended public worship, and took his place with the choir as usual. And on Monday morning he sent, by the hand of his friend, letters to two young men in Cortland, who he understood were engaged in studying—one of them with a view to the ministry. With scarcely an allusion to his own recent affliction and disappointment, and with his heart intent on doing them good, he thus encourages one, and warns and exhorts the other. To the one he says,

"Dear W——, I feared, when I received your last, that your health never would admit of pursuing your studies. I congratulate you, because now you can direct all your energies to the doing of good in that particular line. I am yet on the sea. It is not decided whether I go to college or not, next fall. It will depend somewhat on my health this summer. But it seems to me that I can never be of much use in any employment except the ministry; and certainly not in that, with feeble health. Oh, that all our ministers had the iron frame of the Roman-catholic priest at ——! I cannot begin to say all I wish to."

To the other, who it appears was not a pious youth, he writes in his usual style of parental anxiety and faithfulness.

"Dear K—— —I am glad to hear you are still going on with your studies. From the time I first knew you, K——, there at Mr. B——'s, and saw your burning desire for knowledge—a thing so uncommon to persons with your advantages—I have heard of you with deep interest. And now, K——, permit me in the few lines I shall write, as a friend who has tried all the *agreeables* and the *disagreeables* of study, to suggest two things of the utmost importance. And the first is, there is danger that ambition will cheat you out of your happiness and out of *your soul.* The honors of this world are mere baubles, and so *every one* has found who has tried them. But *religion* gives the *fullest scope* to the immortal mind, while its pleasures never cloy the appetite. Secondly, don't, as you value your life, study too hard. Eight hours of moderate, six of hard study a day, is enough for any body. The great thing is, to form *a habit* of study, which you can continue without injury to yourself through life. If you were going a thousand miles on a wager, you would not set out on a run.

"Excuse my freedom. Believe me, it is prompted by a sincere interest in your welfare, and *love to you.*

"Your affectionate friend,

"J. D. L."

This fresh attack seemed to present a formidable barrier, if not an insuperable obstacle, in the way of his favorite plan of preparing to enter college in the fall. An agricultural life, as it then appeared to me, was that which his heavenly Father designed that he should follow. If this recent paroxysm proceeded from the cause to which we had attributed it, it would be incurring too great a risk to throw him into a position where, as in the profession of a minister of the gospel, such large drafts, especially on particular occasions, would be made on his mind and heart.

The father and son being then alone for several weeks, conversed freely and familiarly on the subject. Conversations were had with several individuals about farms in the neighborhood, and the best method of proceeding in the case of one who, like John, was in a great measure unacquainted with the practical part of farming.

Prior to my return from the east, John had received a visit from a young friend, a kindred spirit, who, although pursuing his studies in the academy at Homer, was rather feeble in health, and somewhat depressed in view of his pecuniary embarrassments. To him John made the proposition, if it should meet my approbation, to come and spend the summer with him, and to make part of our family, gratuitously. An extract from a letter addressed to this estimable young man will disclose still more of the state of his mind just at this juncture.

"BERKSHIRE, June 27, 1844.

"DEAR WALDO—This don't look much like writing the next week, as I promised to do when you were here. But I assure you, that if I could have given any encouragement that we could study together this summer, my silence would not have been long. The facts are these. I could not write before father came home, because I wanted to ask him whether you could be one of us in the family as well as in the study. When he came home he gave his assent to the plan. But another difficulty now presented itself. The excitement attending our lawsuit, of which you have doubtless heard, was too much for my rickety nerves; and I was seized with one of those attacks of epilepsy which drove me from my studies at the age of thirteen. I hoped I had entirely overcome them; as it was more than three years since the last attack. But it now appeared evident to my friends, that though study might not have been the cause of this attack, my nerves were not strong enough to bear the severe trials which a life of study and of ministerial labor would require. After waiting about a fortnight, in hopes that I could still go on after a little vacation, I yielded to the opinion of my friends, who possessed better judgment than I, and more impartiality, and decided *to give up study.*

"Thus, dear Waldo, are we called upon to resign our most fondly cherished hopes, when they interfere with the designs of our heavenly

Father. If my health had continued good, I should have offered you temptations to come and spend the summer with me, which I hope would have been irresistible. Now, my attention must be turned to the pursuit—I had almost said despicable pursuit—of making money. But no, it is not a despicable pursuit to make money, when that money is consecrated to the Lord, whose stewards we are of every talent which he sees fit to bestow upon us.

"Your affectionate friend,

"J. D. L."

About this time, a neighbor needing some assistance in clearing a fallow—logging, as it is called—the young men in the family proposed to John to take hold and help them, doing what he could. Without sufficiently reflecting on the danger of overtaxing the muscular, as well as mental powers, I gave my consent for John to accept the proposition. The young men, though his nearest neighbors and his intimate companions, were ignorant of his recent affliction and of the necessity of moderation in his labor. With his tow frock and trowsers, he went with them on the hills, and labored;

favoring himself as much as he felt disposed. He thought he grew strong with the daily exercise. And he continued it, with some days of intermission, for about a fortnight; when, on the evening of July 15th, he was again seized with the paroxysm, which however, like the one previous, was comparatively light. In a letter to his brother in New York, dated Berkshire, July 22, he gives the following history of this attack:

"Dear R—— —A week ago Monday evening, I again had a slight attack of that disease which has so often, when I felt the strongest, completely prostrated me. A few weeks ago, A. B—— and his brothers, being about to log up a fallow, asked me to work with them. As I had nothing to employ me at home, but little persuasion was needed, and I went on to the hill with them Tuesday of the week that mother came home. You know that in clearing up land, the trees are first felled and cut into lengths; and when the leaves and branches become dry, they are burnt off, so that the blackened logs alone remain. After these logs have been rolled together in heaps, they are again fired; and when they have been entirely consumed, the land is cleared. The part in which I was helping was the rolling up for the second burning. Pretty hard work, and no mistake. No matter about the black dust, which covers one from head to foot with the negro's skin: that is healthy. And the labor is healthy too, for those that can endure it. But you will see before long that I am not one of that class. Tuesday morning I had not felt very well before I went up. Stood it till dinner-time; but then could scarcely crawl home; and it was not till Friday that I felt well enough to try it again. Friday afternoon went up, and Saturday morning. You have probably heard through aunt B—— how I looked when mother came home. The next week was one of rest to me; the B—— boys were hoeing their corn. But week before last they went again into the fallow. Determined not to be discouraged, I went up too; and worked, with the exception of half a day, from Tuesday till they quit on Saturday. It seemed to me that the more I worked the stronger I grew; and that at last I stood it better than almost any of them. But the bow had been too tightly strung. Monday, after whitewashing most of the day—another new trade I have taken up this summer—I was seized with a fit just after I had finished milking. The attack was slight, but it left me weak; and I don't yet feel as though I could roll logs all day."

These two attacks seemed to baffle our calculations. As the first threatened to cut us off from the hope of ever seeing our son a minister of the gospel; this last presented an obstacle, equally formidable, in the way of his being a farmer. It now became more evident than ever, that undue bodily exertion was as unfavorable for him as inordinate exercise of the mind.

A situation in a store was then thought of for him. It may be proper here to say, that at this time John was exceedingly desirous to engage in something; he said he hardly cared what, but something which he might be able safely to pursue for the remainder of his life. He felt as if he had arrived at an age when he ought to be engaged in something besides *vegetating*.

Mr. W——, from Cincinnati, being providentially in Berkshire just at this time, and becoming acquainted with John, and with his parents' wishes concerning him, invited him to return with him to Cincinnati and be his clerk, offering him favorable terms, so far as compensation was concerned. The situation was one which would in a measure gratify the religious feelings of his heart; Mr. W—— being publisher of the Missionary Herald, and other good books, and the head-quarters of many of the valuable benevolent societies of the present day. On advising, however, with friends in New York, the project was abandoned; but with the encouragement that a situation nearer home, and perhaps still more congenial to his wishes, might be obtained for him.

## CHAPTER VIII.

### VISIT TO THE EAST.

On the 28th of July, John, in company with a family in the congregation on their way to the east, left home with a view of visiting friends in New York and its vicinity, and travelling further east if he felt disposed.

The object to be gained was, to benefit his health; and, if possible, find some situation which he might fill, and in which he might be useful. As I remember saying to him, when he took his leave of us, he went like Abraham, not knowing whither he went, but accompanied by the heartfelt prayer that the God of Abraham would be his guide and protector. Going among friends and relatives who knew his situation, who felt a deep interest in his welfare, and who were abundantly competent to advise him, his parents devolved on him in a great measure the responsibility of deciding on any course for life.

Dr. Waldo, in Berkshire, and also Dr. Goodyear, in Cortland, were pupils of Dr. Ives of New Haven. As both of them had frequently referred to their old instructor as one who, in former times, had been uncommonly successful in cases of epilepsy, and as John had never been in New Haven, I recommended to him to visit the professor; and as commencement was nigh at hand, to go to New Haven on commencement-week, where he would have an opportunity of gratifying his literary taste. And furthermore, inasmuch as he had for years been laid aside from study, and recently been attending to it by himself, and as he might wish to know whereabouts he stood in the classical line, I suggested to him, as I could conceive of no objection which would be made to the course, to go into the examination-room and take his place with the candidates for admission to the Freshman class. This he had better do previously to his seeing Dr. Ives. If he failed in passing examination, he must not trouble himself about it; no injury would result from the trial. If he succeeded, then, in conferring with the doctor as to the effect which different occupations would be likely to have on him, he might inquire respecting the effect of a college life.

After having paused a few days, to visit friends at Little Falls and in New York, he went to New Haven, and, as I understand, passed a good examination.

Few young men, perhaps, have entered the examination-room under circumstances equally embarrassing. Not only was the question undecided whether he should enter college, even if he should receive the certificate of the examining committee, but owing to the recent unexpected attacks of his old disease, he had been prevented from completing his review of studies which had been interrupted for about five years; added to which were his fear of the effect of excitement, and his having no recommendation as to his literary qualifications or his moral character.

On receiving his certificate from the examining committee, he, accompanied by an obliging clerical friend from Binghamton, and Dr. Whelpley, a young physician from New Haven, a relative, went to Dr. Ives in order to state his case to him. The result of this conference, and of other conversations with Dr. Whelpley, was, upon the whole, favorable to a college life. He did not, however, feel himself prepared at that time to decide on trying the experiment. But after visiting some of the curiosities about the college, and attending the exercises of commencement, he returned to New York, with a view of advising with his friends there, and of seeking for some suitable place in a store. With the same views, and also to confirm his health, he visited Stamford, and then Poughkeepsie and Hyde Park. Thus he spent the first four or five weeks of the vacation, looking round for some opening in this wide world, where he might safely and usefully labor for his Lord, and yet unable to decide what was his divine Master's will concerning him.

Among the successful candidates for the Freshman class, were two young gentlemen from Binghamton, whose parents were desirous that John should conclude to enter college, and to take a room with their sons. The father of one of them, an intimate acquaintance and our family physician, requested that John would write to him as soon as he had decided on the course he would pursue; in order that he might make correspondent arrangements for his son. Accordingly, under date of Hyde Park, Sept. 17, 1844, he wrote to this gentleman as follows:

"DEAR SIR—You wish I would let you know when I have decided what course to pursue in relation to going to college. My mind is now made up, that, Providence permitting, I shall enter at the beginning of the coming term, which will be next week. Thursday I hope Henry can come. It will be very pleasant for all three of us, who were together at commencement, to be together through our college course.

"It seems to me that I have decided aright, in determining to go. My mind has been set at rest, by fixing it upon this course. I am free from that anxiety, that restlessness, which before was continually harassing me. And I hope, by proper care of myself, and the divine blessing on my endeavors, to go on without injury to my health. My health is now pretty good, though I cannot endure a great deal. Indeed, I think my nervous system generally is acquiring strength. And it seems to me, that with care I may rub along through life quite comfortably, though I can never hope to be fitted for success in stormy times.

"Your affectionate young friend,

"J. D. L."

It was not, therefore, until the week before the commencement of the term, that he decided to join the class. Extracts from his letters to his parents at this time, showing the character and operations of his mind, may not be unacceptable.

Under date of New York, Aug. 17, he writes,

"MY DEAR PARENTS—The past week has been one of great interest to me. I have been to New Haven, passed my examination without difficulty, and received my certificate which entitles me to enter Yale college. Besides this, I have formed several pleasant acquaintances, seen Professor Silliman's cabinet, and the Trumbull Gallery, and attended, with great pleasure, the commencement exercises.

"Tuesday afternoon, went with Mr. Brace and J. Whelpley to see Dr. Ives. With respect to employment, he thought the ministry would not be safe. He would not advise farming. A store would do, if I did not have to stand too much. A country store might answer. If I was fond of study, and did not find it injure me, by taking it moderately, and paying attention to diet and exercise, I would be as well in college as anywhere, and perhaps better. I should be as likely to be well if studying in college, as to attempt it by myself in the country. And after going through college, many stations could be found in which I could be useful, and at the same time healthy. But if at any time in college my fits should recur, I must throw up books entirely.

"I afterwards had another conversation with Dr. Ives, but I have condensed the two into one. J. Whelpley wondered why I hesitated what to do; thinking that it certainly was best to try the college life. 'A store would do for one whose tastes were for mercantile pursuits, but to me it would soon become a dull monotony; and debarred from improving my mind by reading, or expanding it in any way, I should be preyed upon by melancholy.' I believe I have stated all the important points in my conversations with James, and also with Dr. Ives. From the whole, I have drawn the following conclusions:

"First, I cannot hope to be useful as a minister.

"Second, a farmer's life would be no less injurious to me than a minister's.

"Third, it will not improve my chance of success in any employment, 'to vegetate' another year; for even if my health at that time should appear somewhat better, prudence and moderation *in any employment* will be as much needed *then* as *now*. And these same things, aided by the medicines which Dr. Ives recommended, will be very nearly, if not quite as likely to insure my health now as then, or at any future time.

"Fourth, a life in a store would do for me, particularly a country store; for I do not think with Dr. Whelpley that it would become monotonous, as I should endeavor to change entirely my habits of thought, and become interested in business—to make myself a business man. But,

"Fifth, it will be still better for me to go through college, and habituate myself to study; for this, if indulged in moderately, will have a calming, rather than an exciting influence. And it seems probable, that after I am through I shall be able to find some employment of a literary character, which will be beneficial to me.

"It seems to me that I have fairly come to these conclusions, and my course on paper appears very plain. But I know not how soon my feelings may change, according to the circumstances in which I am placed, or the people with whom I associate; and then my course of reasoning might be changed. In fact it seems as though, whatever decision is made, it will be in a great measure a guess, and if successful, a fortunate guess. These opinions which I have now advanced appear to have more reason in them than any which I have before heard or entertained. Perhaps it is because my feelings better accord with them. I hope to have your judgment upon them when you next write."

A younger brother was at that time a pupil in the Collegiate Institute, Poughkeepsie—an institution under the care of Mr. C. Bartlett, and almost unparalleled in our country for the advantages it affords in the training of youth. This brother had, the winter previous, been led to indulge a hope in Christ, but had not yet made a public profession of religion; and was rather backward in conversing with others about his religious feelings. His uncle's house in Hyde Park is only about five miles from the Collegiate Institute, and the two not having seen each other since this supposed change in the younger, one object which John wished to accomplish by a visit up the river, was to have a free conversation with R—— on the subject of personal piety.

Several interviews were had, in which undoubtedly John was, as usual, faithful and affectionate. Still, however, he was not satisfied; but before leaving his dear brother, put into his hand the following, which is without date or superscription. It bears the impress of his yearning heart:

"DEAR R—— —You know, from the letter I wrote you last winter, how much rejoiced I was on hearing that you hoped you had become a Christian. Though of course I felt anxious for you, as I knew that time only would show the genuineness of the work, and that you were exposed to great temptations to forget serious things; yet I gave myself up to the pleasurable anticipations which flowed in upon me, of your character from that time, and to the hope that you would pursue religion as you do every thing else in which you become interested, with zeal. I even went so far as to anticipate the time when we should next meet; and thought, 'If he has indeed tasted the joyful fruits of religion, and is daily drawing nourishment from them, will not his first thought on seeing me be of the great change which has taken place in him since we last met; and of the fact that while we were always *brothers*, we are now *brothers in Christ?*' I hoped that your reserve in talking upon religion would be gone; and that our feelings and sympathies on this subject would have been the same.

"These feelings lasted till I received your letter. I was pained to see that you said so little in that, and to find that you were so silent to all your friends, even to aunt B—— But I then hoped that the change would show itself in your conduct, and that by and by you would be more free to speak on the subject; for I couldn't think it would be *unpleasant* for a Christian to converse on the subject which ought to stand highest in his estimation. But I was assured that it was really so, that it seemed actually painful to you to converse at all about your own feelings. I had been told so by all I saw, who had an opportunity of knowing; and for this reason I had, in a great degree, given up my expectations respecting our meeting. As soon as I sat down and reflected upon the subject, after having seen you last Saturday, I determined to take some opportunity of letting you know my feelings. I have chosen this way, because I once heard you say that you liked to *read* better than to *talk* upon religion. Though, for my part, I do not see why you and I should not talk as freely on this, as on any other subject.

"What evidences have you, dear R——, that you are a Christian? Did you ever enumerate them? Did you ever take a list of test questions, and try yourself in that way? Still more, Do you have *daily* assurance that your affections are set supremely on heaven; or does your hope depend only on the experience of a few days, last winter? What does this reserve mean? You are not naturally diffident. And even if you were, if you had met with so great a change as you suppose, do you believe you could help speaking of it to your *nearest earthly friends?* I beg you, do not pass lightly over these questions on the plea of no time to spare. In a few weeks, you will probably enter on a business in which you will be less disposed to meditation than you now are. And it is vastly important that before you mix in the worldly, money-making crowd, you should *know* whether you have sought 'first the kingdom of God, and his righteousness.' If you are deceived, and cherish your delusive hope, how awful the consequences! How important, then, to have good evidence. And if you find on examination that you have no such evidence, to rest not till you obtain it.

"Will you not embrace the first opportunity to throw off your reserve, and have a conversation with me, that I may aid you in examining yourself? I will gladly attend to any hint that you desire such a conversation. But if you do not like this, will you write a letter and hand it to me, giving all the evidence that you can think of, and saying as much about your feelings as you can? Particularly, be free with me. Your letter will of course be confined to this subject, but if you write one, do make it as long as possible. Do not put it off either, but *begin* it at least at your first leisure hour. Whether you write or have the conversation, I hope you will not feel unwilling to have me repeat what you say; for your friends, particularly father, mother, and aunts, have a right to know your feelings. And it argues poorly for the gratitude of a person rescued from imminent danger, that he is not willing to express that gratitude to his nearest earthly friends.

"If I could say any thing more to induce you to come up to the mark, and take a stand, a decided stand, on the right side, or to show the importance of your pursuing the self-examination which I have proposed, I would say it: I can only pray to God that you may be *indeed* a disciple of the Saviour.

"If you decide to write, I will let you take a little book which I borrowed of Mr. Ludlow, which will aid you to a thorough self-examination. If we talk the matter over, we will use it in the same way—as a guide.

"Your affectionate brother,

"J. D. L."

R—— had been away to school for four years. The day on which he left us, John felt the separation keenly. And as illustrative of his ardent natural affection, as well as simple, childlike piety, I copy from his journal kept at that time the following characteristic entry, under date of Cortland, Sept. 1, 1840:

"Yesterday morning R—— started for New York with his two aunts, who have been out here on a visit. He is going to spend the winter with aunt B——, and attend school in the university.

"After he had gone, I soon began to feel a desperate loneliness. It seemed to me as though I could sympathize, in some measure, with those who have lost a dear friend. The feeling kept growing upon me all day. Whenever I thought of him, or saw any thing of his, my throat would choke up, and I could hardly speak. Sometimes, indeed often, the tears would come; but I managed to keep those concealed from sight. I felt miserably. In the evening, after the children were put to bed, and I sat down with only father and mother, it seemed lonely indeed. I have often sat down in that way before; but then he was about in the village, and would be home at nine o'clock. I tried to read; but soon became tired—having risen early in the morning, and also having had such a pressure upon my feelings all day. I took a candle and hurried off to bed with my eyes full of tears. When I entered my bed-room, saw the empty bed, and reflected that for the next nine months, and perhaps always, I shall now be obliged to sleep alone—such reflections as these 'capped the climax,' and I fell upon my knees and lifted my heart to God in prayer. I prayed for resignation to his will, that he would take away that lonely feeling, and make me cheerful and happy. I poured out my whole soul before him, and arose feeling that my prayer was answered. My tears were gone, and I undressed myself and went to bed, trusting that God would sustain me. I am afraid I shall still feel lonely some, for a week or two; but very little, compared to what I would have done, for 'the Lord is on my side.'"

For this brother, John ever felt great anxiety. For his conversion he constantly and ardently prayed: and with him, after the period of his leaving us, he kept up an active correspondence. On hearing of the death of a much-loved uncle, Hon. Peter W. Radcliffe of Brooklyn, whose funeral R—— had attended and after whom he was named, John thought it would be a good opportunity of impressing on him important truth. And he sat down, and wrote him the following letter:

"CORTLANDVILLE, Dec. 12, 1840.

"DEAR R—— —Our recent affliction is probably still fresh in your mind; and I have thought that it would be well for you to think of it something in this way. You know uncle Radcliffe was always a great friend to our family, and to you in particular. He is now gone. So it will be with all your friends here on earth. They can be here but a short time. They will soon leave you, one after another, and go to their long home. How important, then, is it that you should have a friend who will never leave you, nor forsake you. Such an one you can have in Jesus Christ. HE is a friend indeed; for the more earthly friends forsake you, the nearer will he appear to you. And when you come to die, while you lose your friends on earth, you will go to dwell with one who as far surpasses them all in every good quality, as the sun surpasses the glow-worm. And there, too, if you do choose Christ for your portion, I trust you will find the most of those friends who have gone before you. So that in fact you cannot be said to have *lost* them, but rather to have *gained* them.

"Another reflection is, death to the Christian can hardly be called *death;* it is rather *birth.* It is just the commencement of his life of eternal happiness. The sinner, at that time, can hardly be said to die; for then he just begins to die. His most important part, his soul, will be for ever, and ever, and ever, continually dying, but never dead. Oh then, if it is so terrible to think of dying *once*, that you try to keep your thoughts from the subject as much as you can, what must it be to feel *eternally* this anguish and pain of dying, without any release in death?"

The tone of his correspondence with R—— was ever like that of a Christian to a beloved son, giving him advice and encouragement in the right path. Who would suppose, on reading the preceding, that it was a communication from a lad of fifteen, to a brother not four years younger? Mark also the parental air of the following, dated,

"SILVER LAKE, Oct. 6, 1843.

"DEAR R—— —Your account of the scene in which you took so prominent a part interested me much. I am exceedingly glad if you are acquiring the command of your temper. I should think it would be a very good rule, never to become so much excited that you cannot speak mildly and deliberately. To a mere man of the world, self-possession is of the highest importance. The philosopher's highest glory is his unruffled temper. But if, as I ardently hope, you mean to form your character after the Christian standard, the first point of attack will be that pride which originates every evil passion. Every instance in which you can remain calm through provoking circumstances, is one step, and a great one, gained. And I am very happy to know that your character has already undergone such a change for the better in this respect."

In this passage, John undoubtedly recommends to his brother one of his own rules of life—a rule, an adherence to which had gained for him at Silver Lake the character of one "not easily provoked."

In the trial at Berkshire to which allusion has been made, though he sustained to the parties no other relation than that of witness for the prosecutors, his sympathies were so much with the defendants that he considered himself as one of them, and insisted on bearing his share of the expense to which they had been subjected. In that trial it is plain, from the effect it had on his health, that his feelings were deeply enlisted and sorely tried. Yet all who were present, even fathers in the church, supposed he felt but little; and were struck with the calmness and deliberateness with which he gave in his testimony, and appeared throughout the whole of the disgraceful transaction.

In another letter to R——, dated Dec. 22, 1843, he writes,

"I am reading Hume's history. Had not you better take up Rollin, or something useful, than the light, trashy reading, with which you say you occupy your leisure hours? You will be sorry in after-life, if you do not. Have you read 'The Young Man from Home?' If so, how do you like it? I wish you would tell me in your next, as fully as you please.

"Your affectionate brother,

"J. D. L."

to tell you, without reserve, my feelings. First, I will say that you are often remembered at home, around the family altar, as are all of us. And I have no reason to doubt, that both father and mother daily ask God in secret to renew your heart. As to myself, I am positive I have thought more of you lately than for some time previous. I have sometimes felt almost afraid to think of your situation, and look forward into eternity. For how could I bear to think of my only brother dying without an interest in the blood of Christ. There is, in the life of almost every person, a point upon which all their future interests turn, both for time and for eternity. It is marked in some, with more, in others, with less distinctness. And often the most trifling incident will turn the scale either for life or for death. It appears to me, that now may be just such a crisis with you. I know not what I can say that you have not heard repeated many times over, to induce you to plant your feet upon the Rock. I can only leave you in the hands of God, with the earnest hope that you will not let this opportunity pass by. If you should, how fearful may be the consequences! How can you bear ever to go away from church, or from the Sabbath-school, Sabbath after Sabbath, when you know that every such opportunity is recorded against you in the book above as lost? Or, how can you bear even to lie down to sleep at night, knowing that another is added to the days of sin and rebellion against God, for which you will have to answer at his bar? The command is, to repent *now*. Not a moment is insured to you. And as moment after moment is rolling by, each one bears a sad tale to heaven of resistance against the infinite love of the Son of God.

"I wish you would write to me, giving me your feelings without reserve. If you wish it, no one else will see your letters, not even father and mother, as I am now away from home. —— is indulging hope. One and another around us are coming to the ark of safety: and how long shall I be pained and grieved at the thought that my own dear brother is still holding out against the offers of mercy? Will you not burst the bands of sin, and 'seek first the kingdom of God, and his righteousness?'"

No sooner was he settled at Silver Lake, than he again addressed his brother, under date of Aug. 2, 1843; and after occupying a full half sheet in giving him an account of the exhibition at Homer, etc., he proceeds:

"And now, R——, to other matters. I am again where your letters will be private; and as we are both at an age when our characters are forming for life, we certainly can afford to joke a little less in our letters to each other, and spend the paper and time to better advantage. . . . . . Do you not want a room to yourself, for a time, each day? It cannot be that you have forgotten aunt B——'s instructions, and mother's also, so much as to neglect daily secret prayer.

"The winter I spent in New York, our ever-watchful mother wrote for me the following, which at the time I thought but little of, and threw it carelessly into my Virgil. Now, I prize it as gold. And I send it to you, thinking you will prize it also; and hoping that you will apply it, not only to the case mentioned above, but to every case where right and wrong are involved: 'Whatever conscience tells you is right, that do, and leave the consequences with God; and always remember, THOU GOD SEEST ME.'

"I want to speak of another thing, dear R——, and you must not be impatient at it. You undoubtedly have many temptations, and see and hear many things to excite *evil lusts. Beware how you yield to temptation.* A deadlier vice does not exist, nor one which more debases the body, destroys the soul, and kills every feeling of self-respect; in a word, makes one so completely miserable. When I look back upon the pit from which I have scarcely escaped—if indeed by God's grace I have escaped at all—I shudder; and every feeling of my heart rises for my dear brother. . . .

"Write as soon as convenient. And do, dear R——, devote as much space as you can spare to the subject which you know interests me most. Any of your troubles, if they are worth writing about, will find in me sympathy and confidence."

The preceding are a specimen of his communications with his younger brother. I have examined the whole of the correspondence on his part, and through the whole of it I do not find a line which his pure spirit, now in heaven, need wish to have effaced. And yet, although nearly every letter has something for Christ in it, the reader must not suppose that the communications have nothing else in them. They are interesting as a journal of passing events, in which he supposed R—— would be interested; and some of them are quite of the humorous kind. The account of his school in Berkshire, as found on pages 70–73, was addressed to him. And in that account, from the manner in which he speaks of "trust in Christ," may be seen, not only the avidity with which he would seize on every opportunity to recommend religion to his friends, but the facility, the grace with which he could make a transition to it; perhaps, as in the case before us, only to drop a word, and then to pass on to the topic before him—enough, however, to show where his heart is. Another illustration of the same point occurs at the close of a letter to his brother, dated at Little Falls, July 30, 1844:

"As far as I know, I am well; though my disease is so deceptive that I never can trust my feelings. When I feel the strongest, you know, I am often most in danger.

"Let me apply this principle to a different subject for a moment. If you and I, dear R——, are Christians, we shall find it just so with our hearts. 'When' we are 'weak, then' are we 'strong,' through Christ; but when we have the most self-confidence, then is the time for us to be alarmed. But, good-night. I ought not to have left this subject till the last. But now I shall have to leave off. Shall probably see you in the course of a month or so.

"Your affectionate brother,

"J. D. L."

From the preceding we may infer how great was his anxiety for R——'s conversion; what joy the intelligence of that event must have communicated to his heart, as well as among the angels; and how ardently he *now* longed to see him "come up to the mark," and be a decided, active Christian.

The following incident occurred the day he heard of his conversion. He was then residing at Silver Lake.

The family at the Lake had just disposed of

an immense stock of wool, the clip of two or three years, and valued at nearly $10,000. On receiving a check on the bank of Ithaca for $3,000, the eldest son came with it into the room where John was sitting, and holding it up before him said, "There, John, what do you think of that?" John read the check. It so happened that the same mail had brought the letter from his parents apprizing him of the joyful news of his brother's hopeful conversion; and taking the letter, he held it up before his young friend, saying, with a countenance expressive of a heart full of tender emotion, "There; I have just received here what I would not exchange for your check of three thousand."

It may not be improper to add here, that this younger brother, shortly after John's death, became a member of the Mercer-street church, New York. And there is reason to believe that this letter, and the last conversations of his brother, since departed, have not been lost upon him.

## CHAPTER IX.

### ENTERS YALE COLLEGE—HIS DEATH.

John entered college at the opening of the term. He went alone to New Haven, and made his purchases and arrangements agreeably to his own inclinations, guided by his own judgment. But Providence seemed to raise up friends for him. Wherever he went, it was his happiness to be beloved.

In the spring of 1840, he accompanied me to Philadelphia. And while the General Assembly were in session, we both, having been kindly invited by my esteemed friend and classmate, Hon. Joel Jones, made his house our home. Mrs. Jones, taking a deep interest in my son, requested him to write to her after his return home. In compliance with this request, John wrote to her a letter, in which, after giving an account of one of his attacks, and expressing thanks for the kindness of friends in Philadelphia, he sends several messages to individuals, and among them this: "Please give my love to S——, and tell him that I regret that I said so little to him when I was there, on the subject of religion. I have regretted it ever since, and have prayed over it; and I hope God has forgiven me. But what I did say to him will be sufficient to be a swift witness against him, if, in the great day of accounts, he is not found on the right hand of the Judge."

In a letter of condolence from Mrs. Jones, she expresses the hold which the dear child had taken of her heart, in the following tribute: "His Christian attainments were very remarkable; and his heavenly-mindedness was always apparent. To *me* he was an interesting and profitable companion; so gentle, so frank, so affable, so unobtrusive, and yet always ready, when called upon, to contribute his share to the general fund of conversation. He seemed deeply imbued with the spirit of the gospel. . . . . He was a lovely, lovely youth; and if so lovely to a stranger, what must he have been to a parent's heart?"

During his first visit to New Haven, in commencement-week, he, a stranger, experienced some difficulty in finding a place to board. He was received at length into a family where a few students were accustomed to board; and when about to leave, he asked for his bill: he was surprised to find that the family would receive nothing pecuniary from him as a compensation. And now, on his second visit, though alone, and in an uncommon degree unprepared for a winter's absence from home, and more for entering on a life in college, he was not only favored by friends, but ingratiated himself into the good-will even of strangers. Mr. and Mrs. H——, parents of one of the young gentlemen from B—— before alluded to, providentially found him; and having accompanied their son for the purpose of seeing him comfortably fixed in his new situation in college, kindly advised John, and succeeded in effecting the arrangement which had been desired by *them* and the parents of the other student from B——. The three youths were pleasantly situated in the private family of Mr. Ives, in York-street.

On Saturday, Sept. 28, John wrote to his parents as follows: "The first leisure time I have had I improve to give you some account of myself. I know how anxious you must feel, as I came so unprepared for a settlement. It is indeed almost a wonder to myself that I have succeeded as well as I have, coming as I did without a single article of furniture, with scarcely an article of clothing suitable for winter, and more than all, with my most important books, grammars and dictionaries, at home. But amidst all the confusion of getting settled, buying furniture, and arranging matters, I have been providentially enabled to keep in a great measure free from excitement. The weather has become cooler, just in the right time; so that I have been enabled to do much more than I could in the summer, and with far less danger. . . . . Our tutors are all pleasant and capable, and the class appears to be a pleasant one. . . . . Give my love to the children; and tell them, that if brother John is spared to reach home next summer, he will expect to see them all greatly improved in every respect.

"Your affectionate son,

"J. D. L."

For the remainder of the memoir of my child, I can do little else than let him tell his own story; and this will be brief. Four more communications were received from him; in the first of which, dated October 5, he says,

"I am becoming quite accustomed to the college routine. For exercise, I have kicked football a little; but find it too violent, and mean to quit it *in toto.* Walking is the best exercise I can take. My health continues good by drinking a glass of Congress water every morning. My cold does not trouble me much. But whenever I go into a room where I breathe confined air, I have a troublesome tickling in my throat. I believe, however, this is rather a nervous affection than any thing else; for I scarcely ever raise any thing. I go to bed, as father recommends, in good season. I never study after nine, and am almost always in bed before the clock strikes ten. Charles' alarm goes at five, so that I have seven hours for sleep. I had thought that I could not do with less than eight; but if I once become accustomed to it, I suppose seven will be enough. I think I feel more and more the necessity of the greatest care, to keep from attempting too much before my college habits are firmly fixed. . . . . Our class prayer-meeting comes on Tuesday evening; so I shall almost feel myself at home. Another thing which often causes me to think of Berkshire, the college choir use the 'Carmina Sacra,' and often sing familiar tunes. I should endeavor to join the choir, were it not that they meet every Saturday afternoon for rehearsal; and I do not like the idea of 'signing away my liberty' of Saturday afternoon."

October 19, he again writes, "My health has been pretty good. To be sure, I daily take sometimes Congress water, and sometimes a pill. But then I console myself by thinking, that I could find, in all probability, no place where this would not be necessary, at least for some months; that in every other respect I am better off than I could be anywhere else; and that even if I should always be obliged to do in this way, I would still prefer college life to any other. But in all probability my habits will be formed before long, perhaps by next term; so that I shall not require any medicine. My spirits are almost uniformly good: lessons easy, and I hope before long to get some time to read. As to honors, I think I may truly say, I am not *at all* anxious about them.

"We have several good scholars, really thorough; and the tutors will make us all so, if possible. They are generally very faithful. Evening prayers is generally a very interesting time to me. We have excellent singing by the college choir. The other evening they sung 'Naomi,' to words quite appropriate; and it almost made me choke. They have also lately sung 'Meribah,' 'Brattlestreet,' 'Seir,' 'Hamburg,' and others, which seemed peculiarly *my* tunes, from their associations. . . . . My hour for being in bed is nine o'clock. I stop studying at half-past eight. This is necessary, because Charles' alarm goes at five. At first, I tried being in bed at ten. But I soon found all the unpleasant feelings arising from want of sleep; and when I changed the hour, I felt so much better, that I was ready to exclaim, 'Eureka.' I am very much obliged to you for having inquired so particularly about the family at the Lake. I still feel the deepest interest for them; and hope and pray that those boys may yet be brought under the influence of the gospel of peace."

Nov. 13, he writes, "My health, I think, is gaining. I am the most troubled with those twitchings of the nerves which have troubled me before; but I think I am improving in that respect. My head is generally clear for study; and my stomach, with proper care of my food, in good order. It seems as though it would be impossible to find a place better for me than this; and that if I fail here, I shall be utterly at a loss. The greatest danger is that of being led on to attempt too much; and against this I mean carefully to guard. I commenced teaching a class in Dr. Bacon's Sabbath-school last Sunday; but think I shall give it up, as it takes from me that *rest* which I so much need. I find, however, that I do not feel so well, to sit in my room all day; and have about come to the conclusion, that it can do no hurt to take a walk for exercise, as I do every day. But still, I have some doubts respecting it. Can you tell me what I ought to do?

"Though there are great temptations in college, yet if a person puts himself in the way of the religious influence, *that* also draws with great force. The frequent prayer-meetings, and the fervent exhortations of the professors on Sunday evenings, seem almost irresistible by one who puts himself in the way of them."

The extract which follows will not be understood without some explanation. It is an apology for accepting the office of church committee; and an assurance that, though he had accepted it, his speculative views of duty remained the same as they were before.

The acceptance of the appointment needed no apology. The necessity for making it arose unquestionably in his mind in consequence of a conversation which passed between us shortly after the unexpected attack on the night of the 25th of the preceding May. Being then alone with him for several weeks, I conversed with him freely, and endeavored—whether justifiably or not is a question—to turn his thoughts into a new channel.

It is presumed that every reader of the preceding narrative will believe me, when I say, that from the period of his early conversion, it was never *once* necessary to urge on him attendance to religious duties. Sometimes I have felt as though parental influence might, with propriety, be interposed to restrain him in his attendance on meetings, and efforts to do good. But never did I venture to express to him my thoughts on this point, till at the time above alluded to. Then, presuming that his health would require him to engage in agriculture, and aware that his attention to the subject would be required; and also that then, as it had been for years, his heart was all engaged in ideas of laboring for the good of others, I endeavored to impress on him the necessity of letting go this anxiety for others, as though the whole world was resting on his shoulders, and of feeling that, as an inhabitant of this earth, he had a work to do in taking care of himself. Never before had I been situated where I felt myself called on to take this position. But I felt at the time that duty to my son required it. And now I can only express the hope and prayer, that at the great last day, when we both shall meet, it may not appear that I acted the part of "Mr. Worldly Wiseman," instead of a truly Christian parent.

The extract alluded to is from the last letter which was superscribed by his own hand, written Saturday evening, Dec. 1, and is as follows:

"I delivered father's letter from the church to one of the members of the senior church committee, and to-day it was read the first time before the church. I have been chosen by my class-mates as a member of the church committee. Thus you see they are drawing me into the harness. After I became convinced that I could not be a minister, I felt sensibly the effect of my change of purpose upon my spirituality; more particularly upon my interest in the conversion of others. And when I came here, I felt like resting from care for the good of others, as well as from every other care; and living as the great majority of Christians do. I believe, that from the very importance of the subject, this kind of care is more likely to wear upon a person than any other. I know that it has often borne heavily upon me. One great reason against my becoming a minister is, that in that station such anxiety would be so likely to overwhelm me. And though the worth of souls is great as it is, yet I cannot believe it my duty to spend half a dozen years perhaps, in directly laboring for them, and then die; when by taking care of myself, and doing what I could in other ways, I would have a reasonable prospect, under God, of being spared to accomplish much more in the end than I otherwise could. With these views I came to college. Indeed, I feel much in the same way now. That is, I have much the same views of duty; but did not see how I could refuse the election of my classmates. The vote for me was larger than for any one of the others who were chosen; and if I should decline, I did not see whom they would choose from our division. When I look at it, the responsibilities of even this office are tremendous. But I mean to endeavor to keep as much as possible from thinking of these; and to do what I can, from time to time, as calmly as I perform any of my accustomed tasks. A great deal is expected here of a member of the church committee. He must watch over the spiritual interests of his division, much as a pastor does over his flock; and report once in two weeks to the general committee, composed of the committees from all the classes. I have made a beginning in finding out the spiritual character of the members of our division; and hope, by system, to keep an eye upon them all: and yet not do so much as to wear upon my health."

The next was commenced by John, but finished after his death by his afflicted friend and room-mate. It is dated Dec. 14, and commences as follows:

"Dear Father—I commence a letter a week earlier than I otherwise should, because the two remaining Saturdays of the term are devoted to writing prize translations; and I am anxious to have time enough to do our friend the 'Excerpta' full justice, without being hurried.

"The most important news I have to tell you will not, I fear, be very welcome. I have had another fit. A week ago last Thursday, just after eating a hearty dinner, and finishing off with a liberal piece of mince-pie, I was commencing my Latin lesson, when I was seized with the convulsions. From all I can learn, I was attacked as I always am; but, as I have been for the three or four last times, with comparatively little violence. I was treated with the greatest kindness, not only by the family, but by all my class-mates who heard of it. Several were in to see me; and some, two or three times. I did nothing the next day at my regular lessons; and nothing of consequence on Saturday. Monday, feeling pretty well, I began again; and have kept on all this week. And now I think I can say without presumption, I am better than I have been in a long time. I have daily feared lest this new state of my system should be interrupted; but still it continues. How much longer it will, my heavenly Father only knows. But I trust in him, that as I think I followed the leadings of his providence in coming here, he will permit me to stay.

"You may ask, why I did not immediately leave, or at least write home, and cease from studying till I should receive an answer. I doubt whether I could have done the last, as I was not actually sick, so as to prevent my studying. The reason why I did not leave at once, or write home immediately, is the same, namely, I had strong reason to believe the attack was not caused by study. Dr. Ives laid it to the mince-pie. Perhaps it was partly that; but there must have been some other causes. It seemed very clear to me, and Dr. Ives said so too, that the attack could easily be accounted for without laying it to study. Indeed my studies, for the week or so previous, had been rather light. We were reviewing in algebra; and the other studies were not very hard. I therefore concluded, that as I had just sent off a letter to you, I would say nothing more about it till my regular time for writing again; and in the mean time, begin studying when Dr. Ives should think it safe, and adopt all possible measures of security for the future. The result thus far has been, as I said before, encouraging beyond my hopes. And it seems to me that I can with safety continue my experiment at least for a time. Vacation is now near at hand; when an opportunity will be afforded to obtain new vigor for another campaign."

The remainder of the sheet is filled up by his room-mate, and is as follows:

"New Haven, Dec. 21, 1844.

"Rev. Mr. Lockwood—It remains for another hand to finish the epistle of your departed son. John has gone! Suddenly he was snatched from us, and carried, as we have full reason to believe, by angels to Abraham's bosom. He tells you the state of his health down to the time when he was writing. He took a severe cold within a few days; and Wednesday he was almost laid up with it. His head and throat seemed to be choked up with catarrh. He attended the two morning recitations, however. At noon I found he had some fever. Although I did not apprehend any serious illness, I asked him if I had not better call in Dr. Ives. He said, no; that he should try to sweat it off at night. We put a bed in our warm room; and having bathed his feet in hot water, and taken warm drinks, he retired. The next morning, on asking him how he had rested, he said it seemed to him that he had not slept at all. After breakfast, with a reluctant consent from him, I went for Dr. Ives. He promised to come immediately after his lecture, at ten o'clock. He accordingly came, and made one or two prescriptions. He said John had considerable fever. At night the doctor came again, found his fever quite high. He said he calculated to have him sleep that night; and gave him a powder to that effect, as I suppose. John retired to bed pretty early, his drinks by his bedside; and was requested to call us if he wished for any thing. Yesterday morning we found he had had a very restless night. Dr. Ives came in after breakfast; said John was very sick, and left new prescriptions, which were administered according to his directions. Dr. Ives came in again at noon, and said that he would call again in the evening. By this time John began to grow rather wild. He had been a little so at times in the forenoon. In the evening one of the tutors came in to see him. . . . . The doctor not coming very early, I went after him. He had quite severe paroxysms after Drs. Ives and Whelpley left; but he gradually grew more quiet. We continued to give him his medicines; but he seemed to breathe with more and more difficulty. I saw this, and was about starting for Dr. Whelpley, when he came in, and said John was dying. At a quarter past twelve he breathed his last, without a struggle. He has complained of no pain from the beginning.

"Yours in haste,

"H. S. WEST."

The class, on being made acquainted with this sudden breach upon their number, met and passed the following preamble and resolutions, namely:

"Whereas, by an afflictive dispensation of Providence, we are called to mourn the death of our beloved class-mate and friend, who had endeared himself to us by his amiable character and sincere piety:

"*Resolved*, That we deeply sympathize with the parents and friends of the deceased.

"*Resolved*, That as a mark of our sorrow, we wear the usual badge of mourning for thirty days.

"*Resolved*, That a copy of these resolutions

be transmitted to his parents; and also that they be published in the New Haven papers, the New York Observer, the Binghamton Courier, and Republican."

The parents take this opportunity to acknowledge with gratitude the receipt, not only of the preceding, but also of an affectionate expression of sympathy from the pen of Wm. K. Mehaffey, appointed to forward them.

From the preceding extracts of John's letters while in college, it appears that, in compliance with the injunctions of his parents, and the recommendations of physicians, he denied himself the satisfaction of applying his mind to study as many hours as his inclination would have craved. His parents having a circle of relatives and other friends in New Haven, he was desired to become acquainted with them. From his letters to us, it appears that he was in the habit of calling upon some of them already, and that it was his intention to enlarge his acquaintance of this sort. If he visited more than is common among students, he did so, not because he had an aversion to study, but as a matter of relaxation and of duty, to gratify his parents, and to guard his health.

On Saturday morning his afflicted room-mate went to all those relatives in town, with whom he knew John had formed an acquaintance, and apprized them of his death. With hearts bleeding with grief and sympathy for the bereaved, they not only repaired to his boarding-place and superintended all the arrangements necessary for a decent burial, but several of them, spontaneously and without concert, despatched letters to his relatives in the city of New York, apprizing them of the event.

Communications from some of those friends since his death not only confirm the report which from time to time our son gave us, but express the feelings of satisfaction with which those calls of his were regarded, and even anticipated. One of them, addressed to Mrs. Lockwood, is as follows:

"New Haven, Dec. 21, 1844.

"My dear Cousin—You may easily imagine how we were shocked this morning, when a messenger called to inform us of your darling son's death. Every evening this week, we had been anticipating a promised visit from him; and every time the front-door bell rang, some one of us would exclaim, That is cousin John. And last evening when some friend called, imagining it was his well-known step I heard, I went to meet him. Fearing he was not as well as usual, as he did not call last evening, I had intended to-day to request sister M—— to let their man call and see if sickness had prevented him. So we had previously done, when he has failed of making his habitual weekly call. Last Friday evening, the last time he came to see us, just a week before he died, he seemed very cheerful, but appeared to have a slight cold, or influenza. I then requested him to let us know immediately if he felt any worse, that we might administer to his wants or necessities; at the same time telling him I should never forgive him if he did not let us know, as he might suffer for the want of proper attention. He told me he certainly would let me know if he were sick; but remarked he was sorry he caused his friends so much anxiety. I have been down twice to-day, and have seen Mrs. Ives, with whom he boarded. She seems sincerely afflicted at this painful dispensation of Providence; and I have not the least doubt has done every thing in her power to alleviate his sufferings. Indeed, she told me he never admitted that he suffered the least pain. Dr. Whelpley told me that he was with him until his last moment, that he finally seemed to rest in sleep when his spirit, as a bright gem, went to deck his Saviour's crown. The casket, beautiful, is left. And O, what a placid and sweet expression—so much like life! And surely that expression was an index of his soul.

"I have reserved some of your son's hair. I will send it by some of your friends from New York, whom we expect to attend the funeral."

The following tribute is from another, dated New Haven, January 7, 1845, and addressed to Mrs. Lockwood:

"If, my dear cousin, you believe with me, that not one iota of intellect or acquisition is lost, that all enlargement of mind, all knowledge gained, if rightly used and consecrated to the service of the Redeemer, goes with its possessor to the world above, to fit him for a higher station there, you will not lament John's diligent and successful study, during his sojourn here.

"You will be glad to learn that he won golden opinions from all who knew him. I have made diligent inquiries of the young men I know, those who did not sympathize in his higher aspirations, as well as those who did, and from all I have heard the same testimony of respect and regard. He was, I am told, the first scholar in his division; but over and above all was the influence of his religious character. —— —— told me that he had never known a death in college produce so general an effect as your dear son's; and he hoped the result would be such as to afford much comfort to his friends."

From other sources gratifying information has been received, not only in reference to his standing in his class as a student, but in the college as a Christian. The unanimity with which his fellow-students elected him as one of the church committee for his class, affords some proof of the confidence which they were willing to repose in him.

His parents value as a treasure the following

testimonial, recently communicated to them from one of his associates of the church committee; and which, as one of the tutors who has read it informs me, "expresses," he has no doubt, "the views and feelings of his class-mates generally."

"As a scholar, he stood high in the estimation both of his teachers and class-mates. The general voice of the men of his own division had placed him among the first in his class. Yet, if we may judge from his own actions and manner, his aim was not to surpass others, but to attain to excellence. His ambition was not that of rivalry, but of high purpose. In his studies as well as in other things, he evidently kept in view the great end of his being, the glory of God.

"His character as a man was unblemished in the eyes both of his fellow-Christians and of the irreligious. I have never heard the charge of inconsistency brought against him, even by those who always judge harshly of Christian character. His influence was always on the side of right and decorum. No one thought of looking to him for aid in any scheme of disorder, or disregard to college authority; yet he was never backward in giving his influence in favor of any plan of usefulness. He took an active part in the formation of the class Temperance Society, of which he was chosen president, though he did not see fit to accept the office. He had about him an air of stability, and of innate dignity, which commanded the respect of all who knew him. He had nothing of that levity which destroys the influence of so many professors. The general expression of his countenance indicated a cheerful sobriety of disposition; though the state of his health, which was poor all the while he was in college, sometimes gave him an air of languor. Often before his last sickness, and especially since his death, have I heard from the pious members of our class, remarks showing their attachment to him, and their confidence that his influence would always be in favor of religion and order.

"But we love most to think of him as a Christian. His piety was of that humble, consistent stamp which, without obtrusiveness, is evident to every one. No person who has spent a day in his company would fail to discover it.

His piety was that of the heart. His affectionate disposition and gentle dignity of manner often enabled him to introduce the subject of religion to the attention of those who scorned to listen to it from the lips of others. His manner of conversing with the impenitent convinced them that he was impelled to do so, not merely by a sense of duty, but by a heart tenderly alive to their best interests. He was accustomed to take part in almost all our class prayer-meetings. His prayers were characterized by humility, a sense of sinfulness and dependence, trust in God, and confidence in the worthiness and ability of the Saviour. His exhortations were usually on subjects suited to warm the Christian's heart, and encourage him in the path of duty. I well recollect some of his last addresses. On the last Sabbath before his death—he died on Friday night—he spoke to us on the uncertainty of life; making it a motive to the Christian for greater activity in the service of Christ; little thinking at the time how soon his remarks would be verified in his own experience. And on the succeeding Tuesday evening, at a prayer-meeting in my room, he addressed us on the subject of the goodness of God; particularly as shown by our constant preservation: saying, 'Every beat of the pulse is a blessing from God. In this way alone we receive at least sixty blessings every minute; in an hour, sixty times as many; and in a day, a year, a vast multitude.' Then laying his fingers upon his wrist he exclaimed, 'Oh, how good is God, to preserve us in being for a single moment!' I remember these expressions the more distinctly, because they were the last I ever heard him utter. We had hoped to enjoy his society for years to come; but God in his wisdom and goodness had planned for him better things.

"JOS. ROWELL."

The funeral was attended on the afternoon of the Monday succeeding his death. It was near sunset by the time the congregation were assembled in the chapel; and several who were present have remarked on the impressiveness of the few religious exercises on that occasion; particularly on the tender expression with which the following touching hymn of Bishop Heber was sung by the college choir:

"Thou art gone to the grave, but we will not deplore thee,
Though sorrows and darkness encompass the tomb;
The Saviour has passed through its portals before thee,
And the lamp of his love is thy guide through the gloom.

Thou art gone to the grave—we no longer deplore thee,
Nor tread the rough path of the world by thy side;
But the wide arms of mercy are spread to enfold thee,
And sinners may hope, since the Saviour hath died.

Thou art gone to the grave—and its mansions forsaking—
Perhaps thy tried spirit in doubt lingered long;
But the sunshine of heaven beamed bright on thy waking,
And the song that thou heard'st was the seraphim's song.

Thou art gone to the grave—but 'twere wrong to deplore thee,
When God was thy ransom, thy guardian, and guide;
He gave thee, and took thee, and soon will restore thee,
Where death hath no sting, since the Saviour hath died."

In consequence of this sudden death, an unusual solemnity seemed to rest on the minds of the students; and the friends of Christ abroad who knew John, prayed most earnestly that the Spirit of God might descend as a copious shower on that venerated institution. The members of the church and the officers of the college, for a time, felt greatly encouraged to hope that this blessing was about to descend. Vacation, however, which commenced within ten days after the funeral, though it lasted only two weeks, dissipated in a measure the serious impressions which an event so affecting was suited to excite. Although no general revival of religion was experienced in the college, the friends of Christ have reason to believe, that both in the institution and elsewhere the dispensation was blessed to the good of souls.

As another testimonial of the affection and respect with which the class regarded John, they resolved to erect a monument to his memory. Their first design was to procure a stone, the cost of which was one hundred and twenty dollars. It is one of the wise regulations of the college, that in cases of this sort the faculty must be consulted, and their consent obtained. In this case the faculty approved of the resolution of the class to erect a monument; but objected, mainly in view of the injurious tendency of the precedent, to the amount to which they were about to tax themselves, and restricted them to sixty dollars.

The monument, which stands in the new college lot, in the north-west part of the city burying-ground, is a plain, four-sided column of Italian marble, five feet in height from the block of granite on which it stands; gradually tapering to the capital, which projects three or four inches. On one side of the shaft, is the following inscription:

JOHN D. LOCKWOOD,

A MEMBER OF THE

FRESHMAN CLASS, Y. C.

SON OF REV. PETER LOCKWOOD,

OF BERKSHIRE, N. Y.

DIED DECEMBER 20, 1844.

ÆT. 19.

---

ERECTED BY HIS CLASS-MATES.

---

Mrs. Lockwood and myself have once visited the spot. It was late on the afternoon of Saturday preceding commencement-week. Lingering there, we became interested in deciphering the inscriptions on two old tomb-stones, which stood at the head of our son's grave, and which told us who were his neighbors in that house appointed for all the living. The nearest reads thus: "In memory of that amiable and pious youth, Wm. Joseph Sweetland, of Hebron, a student at Yale College, who departed this life, August the 20th, 1776, in y[e] 19th year of his age." The other on a stone adjoining, reads as follows, namely, "Here lies the body of Israel, the son of Hezekiah Brainerd, who died, a member of Yale College, Jan. 6, 1784. Ætatis Suæ 23."

We took this last to be for the brother of David Brainerd the missionary. We wiped our tears, and came away.

"O the depth of the riches both of the wisdom and knowledge of God! how unsearchable are his judgments, and his ways past finding out!" This exclamation of an apostle, though penned originally in view of that dispensation of divine Providence by which the Jews were rejected and the Gentiles called, presents itself as appropriate in view of the series of dispensations in reference to the life, the death, and the burial of this beloved son. To say nothing now of his life and death, I am struck with the view of the ways of God derived from a consideration of *his burial-place.*

On his mother's side, John Davenport Lockwood was a descendant, in the seventh generation, of the Rev. John Davenport, who was the first minister of New Haven. If John gloried in any thing of an earthly nature, it was in his being a lineal descendant of this puritan ancestor. Among his manuscripts sent to us from New Haven, is "A Genealogy of the Davenport Family in America," obtained by him from some source during his residence in college.

God loves to honor his children. "Them that honor me, I will honor," is his language. Had the question been asked John while in health, where he would prefer that his body should repose till the resurrection, he might have considered the question as improper, and would have answered, if he answered at all, that it was a subject to which he had not given a thought; that it matters but little where the body is laid, if the soul is only at rest with God in heaven. Sure I am, if any one had pointed out to him the spot where his remains now lie, in the cemetery of New Haven, ornamented and pleasant, beneath a monument erected by mourning and beloved class-mates, and among a group of college students who, like him, had died away from home, he would have considered himself unworthy the honor proposed to be put on him. With characteristic modesty he might have turned away his face and wept, thinking within himself, but "who am I, or what is my father's house?" Sure I am, that in his estimation, the most distinguished niche in Westminster Abbey would have borne no comparison with the ground where his remains now lie. When I think of his loosing from his parents under the embarrassing circumstances which have been detailed; then floating for weeks, unable to ascertain the will of his heavenly Father, and uncertain in what direction to steer his course, and then anchoring his bark in *New Haven*, I cannot but ask myself in admiration of the ways of Providence, did the God whom he served waft him to my beloved Alma Mater, and give him the hearts of his teachers and associates, in order that He might honor him with so desirable a resting-place in *the home of his fathers' sepulchres?*

# CHAPTER X.

## SUMMARY.

Enough, perhaps, has been said; and yet I cannot lay down my pen without endeavoring to sketch a miniature likeness of John, as he appeared in the different stages of his life, and under the different circumstances in which, by the providence of God, he was placed.

And, 1. *John in the nursery.* One effect on my own mind of the compilation of these memoirs has been, to bring his infantile form before me. I can now see him, the little boy, amusing himself with blocks. Nothing that his parents could get for him would interest him so uniformly, and for so long a time, as a set of blocks, which he could put together in the shape of houses or castles, and then knock them down again. And after he commenced the study of geography, he would amuse himself by laying them out in the form of rivers, etc. During the season for flowers he is tracking his way through the grass, picking the dandelions, and hastening to show them to his mother and all the family, exclaiming, "Pretty dans, pretty dans." In the nursery, he was a happy child. Now methinks his little voice sounds in my ear, as during his hours of play he attempts to express his happiness in a monotonous sort of tune. For, though he was fond of music, he was not a natural singer; though in after-life he succeeded in obtaining a knowledge of the science of music, and learned to play a little on the flute, and always sung in the family, and in latter years had a place with the choir, he never probably would have succeeded in being an accomplished singer. The only time when I recollect seeing him weep over any difficult task, was when he was first attempting, with others, to learn to sing. He could master the theory, and every thing which he could *see.* But there was something more, something which depended on the *ear;* and the sounds would not come out right to the *ear.*

2. *In the family.* And here he was all that his parents could wish a child to be: obedient

and respectful towards *them*, and affectionate towards his brother and sisters. He was always orderly and quiet in the house; cheerful himself, and doing all in his power to make those around him so. He was ever ready to assist where he could be of any use. Each of his three little sisters was taught to read by him; and from him acquired the first rudiments in arithmetic. And they loved to be under their elder brother's instruction.

Possessed of information uncommonly varied and extensive for one of his years, and being naturally of a lively turn, he was an agreeable companion for the parlor or the evening fire-side.

3. *In the school-room.* Here he was a pattern for boys; diligent and persevering in his studies, respectful to his teacher, and kind and obliging to his companions. As a consequence, he succeeded in his mental efforts, gained the confidence of his teachers, and the good-will of his associates. One trait in his character deserves especial notice, namely, his Christian manner of receiving injuries. When ill-used

by any of his associates, he never retaliated. *I do not remember that he ever once quarrelled with another boy.* Though John understood the English language, and could analyze a difficult sentence in it as well perhaps as any lad of his years, he never attended to the English grammar as a separate study: this he acquired through the medium of the Latin and the Greek. Milton's "Paradise Lost" he studied as a scholar would his Virgil. And not a sentence would he pass till he could understand and analyze it. And in his copy of the work I find a manuscript in lead pencil, being notes on the first ten books, and up to line 545 of the eleventh book; in a few instances noting "obscure" against a passage. As a scholar, he was uncommonly exact, thorough, and mature.

Soon after the issue of the first edition of this work, the following communication was received from Rev. Henry A. Nelson, dated Auburn Theological Seminary, Jan. 8, 1845.

"My dear Sir—I have just read your memoir of your lamented son, loaned me by brother

McKinney. I cannot refrain from immediately expressing to you the gratification I have received from the perusal of the book; and my thanks for your having given us so faithful a portraiture of so engaging a character. I wonder it did not occur to me, when I knew you were preparing this work, that there was an interesting period of his life, in which I had a better opportunity of observing him than any one else. I mean the few months he spent at Homer, during which I was his teacher.

"I still feel disposed to express to you the gratification I experienced from watching your son, and studying his interesting character, during the short time when he was my pupil. His recitations to me were in the Latin and Greek languages. I have never listened to translations from a pupil or a fellow-student with greater pleasure than to John's. I remember, too, the satisfaction with which his class-mates used to listen to his recitations. He had one class-mate much older than himself, and who, as I have often said, possesses more mental vigor than any young man whom I ever instructed. I have often heard him express the delight with which he observed the action of John's mind. His translations evinced sound judgment, refined taste, a vivid perception of the beautiful and sublime in sentiment and language, and a knowledge unusually thorough for his years, of the principles of the Latin and Greek languages.

"His manifestations of moral character were not less pleasing. If he had failed in any instance to apprehend the true meaning of his author, he received the hint which set him right, not with an expression of countenance which denoted chagrin and mortified pride, but with a look which indicated the delight of an ingenuous mind at the discovery of truth. He was grateful for aid in finding a beautiful thought which had eluded his search. His deportment in other respects was characterized by a manifest appreciation of the proprieties of his position as a pupil, and a conscientious regard for them. As he boarded in the same family, he was not only my dutiful pupil, but an agreeable companion. He manifested in his intercourse those traits which you ascribe to him. His mind was always active. In school, he not only studied his text-books, but he studied *his class-mates and teachers.* I remember that in one instance I was severely tried by the conduct of one of his class-mates. In a conversation which afterwards occurred between us, John showed that he had watched the case with intense interest, and as I thought with a clear apprehension of the principles involved. I remember well the kindness and delicacy of feeling which he manifested towards his class-mate, and the delight which he expressed at having learned, as he thought, something of importance respecting the action of mind, and the principles which should be observed in dealing with minds in certain moods.

"The evidence which the memoir gives of his proficiency in botany recalls to my mind this fact. I had paid little attention to this science, and knew only its simplest rudiments. In some of my leisure moments during that summer, I read part of Mrs. Lincoln's work, and in several instances analyzed with John, some of the flowers in Dr. B——'s garden, in which we were wont to spend our moments of relaxation.

John always manifested a deep interest in the subject; but though he was as well fitted to be *my* instructor in botany, as I his in languages, he never displayed this superiority with ostentation. He preferred to converse upon those topics in which his superiority would not appear. We could enjoy together those hints at theological truths of which botany is so fruitful.

"H. A. N."

4. *In the Sabbath-school.* His parents were not solicitous to send him very early to the Sabbath-school. They were unwilling to entrust him at a very early age to any teacher *on the Sabbath-day, and away from home.* When he was about six years of age, however, he became a member of the Sabbath-school in Binghamton; and from that time till the day of his death, with only the slight interruptions occasioned by his temporary absence or indisposition, he was either as pupil or as teacher, heartily and actively engaged in the cause. In the progress of his history I have noted his connection with the Sabbath-schools in Binghamton, in Cortland, in Homer, at Silver Lake,

and his desire to be useful in that way in New Haven. Wherever he went, he never failed to attach himself to a circle of youths, whose welfare he seemed to have deeply at heart. And it is believed that he has never been in a place, even for a short time, and formed acquaintances of this sort, where he is not remembered with unusual interest and affection. Many, connected with the Sabbath-schools where he has lived, may at last rise up and call him blessed.

5. *In the social prayer-meeting*. He never requested to be excused when asked to lead in prayer. And whenever the opportunity was given for remarks, he never suffered the meeting to languish for want of some one to occupy the time. Far from avoiding these sacred circles, he always attended them, unless unavoidably prevented. Whoever else might flag in their attendance, he would be punctual; and generally, in the juvenile meetings, he was requested to take the lead. And while he was ever ready to contribute his share of time and effort to sustain them, and render them inter-

esting, he was by no means considered as offensively obtrusive. If any one else was ready to occupy his place, he was always ready to relinquish it with cheerfulness. He seemed to understand the precept of the apostle, and to act upon it: "In honor preferring one another." Instead of wishing to be foremost, he always strove to promote the advancement of others. For he was taught, among the earliest lessons of his childhood, that the superior worth of others would not lessen his; that the relative inferiority of others would not elevate him in the sight of God; and that his great aim should be, to increase the amount of moral excellence in the universe.

Wherever he has lived, his influence has been felt in bringing forward the youthful members of the church to love the prayer-meeting, and to sustain it by their efforts. Youthful members, encouraged by his example, have overcome their natural reluctance to speak and to pray in public.

John was a believer in the efficacy of prayer. His practice of making particular individuals subjects of his prayers has been alluded to

And it is an encouragement to all those who are copying his example in this respect, to note the cases in which *such* are now professors of religion and exemplary Christians.

6. *In the church.* Though admitted at so early an age into the church, and though in his prayers he always confessed his remissness and wanderings, certain it is, he never went astray so far as to occasion the least anxiety of his parents, or to attract the notice of his brethren. He was a regular and punctual attendant on the preparatory lecture, and on every regularly appointed church-meeting. So far from absenting himself from the communion-season, he was always present. It is believed, that from the time of his first partaking to the close of his life, he did not miss one such season. In the church-conferences and prayer-meetings, and meetings for business, while he never exposed himself to the charge of meddling with matters either too high for him, or belonging to men of adult age and mature experience, he was always ready, whenever any project for doing good was before the meeting, to express

his own opinion, and encourage the hearts of all. He carefully avoided every thing which looked like dictating to others in the church.

He commenced a journal at the time he was eight years old, which, with occasional interruptions, he continued as long as he lived. In this journal the daily exercises of his heart appear, mourning over his unfaithfulness and unprofitableness, and breathing forth desires to be useful.

7. *On the Sabbath.* The whole of this sacred day he used to spend "in acts of public or private worship, except so much as was taken up in works of necessity or mercy." The Sabbath never seemed a weariness to him. On other days he habitually read, as a student, the New Testament critically, in its original Greek. On this day he studied the inspired volume with a view of catching the spirit of it, and reducing to practice what he read.

8. *In affliction.* Early in life he was called to endure pain. He bore this yoke in his youth. But all his other trials were as nothing, in com-

parison with his epilepsy. This threatened to blast all his prospects, and to disappoint all those hopes of usefulness which he had so fondly cherished. He read various medical treatises on the subject. He understood the operation of the disease. He well knew that unless it was checked, it would, sooner or later, make fearful ravages on his mind, as well as on his body. Yet it is believed no one ever heard him utter a murmuring word in view of this afflictive dispensation.

Young persons are generally prone to consult their appetites, and to object to taking medicine, however necessary for their health; or even to deny themselves the satisfaction arising from eating palatable and nourishing food, how much soever the partaking of it would injure them. Young people of his age are very apt to show an unwillingness to undergo any surgical operation which, though for their good, is painful. But not so with John. Though generally blessed with appetite, he was for several years put on a system of dieting, at one time extremely rigid: prohibited from eating not only pies and cakes and sweetmeats, but all rich food. Meat and butter were, at that time, contraband articles. And voluntarily abstaining from tea and coffee, often, while others have been partaking of the bounties of Providence, has he made his meal of bread, or crackers, and water. And for this, it is believed, his heart devoutly and ardently sent up its tribute of thanks to the great Giver. The only expression bordering on dissatisfaction with his lot, or despondency in view of it, which can be recollected, is a remark made several times in Cortland, immediately on recovering his consciousness after attacks for which he could assign no cause: "Well, I must give up. I don't know how to guard against them." There is abundant reason to think that this severe affliction from his heavenly Father was sanctified to him. It made him gentle, calm, collected, as well as subdued and chastened in his temper.

9. *In his active efforts to do good.* One way in which he successfully labored in this field, was by benefiting his young brethren; encouraging them in every good work; kindly exhorting those who needed exhortation, and

faithfully warning those who were in danger of being led astray. By always demeaning himself in the social circle as a Christian, his example was like a bright and shining light to his brethren, who, like him, professed to have put on Christ. He seemed, in some good degree, to feel that the character of his Christian brother was, in an important sense, a part of his own; and over it he therefore practised something of the same watchfulness that he did over his own.

Another way in which he labored to do good, was by gaining access to the hearts and consciences of the impenitent, and endeavoring to influence them to renounce their sins, and to choose Christ. He labored for souls like one who was to give account. And while he thus assiduously labored, he fervently prayed to God in behalf of those same souls; thoroughly conscious of his own impotency and that of others, and firmly convinced of the ability and the willingness of God to interpose for them and save them.

Another way in which John endeavored to do good, was by contributing what he could, by prayer and influence and money, to sustain the prominent benevolent enterprises in which Christians of the present day are engaged. His annual contribution to the American Board of Foreign Missions for some years was five dollars. This was his annual offering, over and above his contributions at the monthly concert. On these occasions he always contributed something—I presume a stated sum, judging from his habits of order. And of these concerts he was sure of attending twelve every year. His regular yearly contributions to the American Tract Society, American Bible Society, American Home Missionary Society, were one dollar a year. To the other benevolent enterprises of the day, such as the Bethel cause, the Sabbath-school cause, and the education cause, he also contributed, whenever those objects were presented.

It ought to be noted, that for several years before his death his contributions for benevolent purposes were from his own funds entirely. And those funds were mostly the fruit of his own earnings. He had deposited sums with me which at his death amounted to $17 75, and which were distributed among eight of our benevolent societies, as it was believed would have been in accordance with his wishes.

10. *As a missionary.* What though he never entered on heathen territory, and was not permitted to enjoy the high privilege which he aspired after, of blowing the gospel trumpet in the hearing of benighted pagans: to this cause he had been consecrated by his parents; to this high calling he dedicated himself with his first Christian breath; and he never seemed disposed to retract his dedication. His chosen field was China. There he would rather have labored than in any other part of the globe. But he held himself in readiness to go anywhere. After epilepsy had come on him, and driven him from his favorite pursuit of knowledge through the medium of books, he seemed willing to increase his stock of information in domestic and other matters. While engaged in duties about the house, or in the cabinet-shop, or in the chair-factory, or in the harvest-field, or at his bench at home, he used to remark pleasantly, that all these things might be

fitting him for certain situations in which, by the providence of God, he might in after-life be thrown. About that time he became interested in reading "The Family Robinson," and would often speak to his mother of the expedients to which he could now resort, in case he should be cast or left on a desolate island. There is reason to believe that he never at any time quite gave up the idea that the great Head of the church would make the way clear for him to labor in his service as a missionary to the heathen. When his mother on one occasion was dissuading him from laboring in the cabinet-shop, his reply to her was, "Mother, suppose I should be situated as Mr. Williams was, on the South-Sea Islands, then all this knowledge would be of use to me." He had *the heart* of a missionary. He was unquestionably regarded as such by God. Why then may not his name be associated with the missionary work in the minds of all who may read this memoir, as it certainly will be in the minds of his bereaved, though not afflicted parents?

And now, beloved son, farewell. In thy lifetime thou wert a great comfort to thy parents;

but not so great as thou hast been since thy sudden departure. Never before could I realize *the amount, the sweetness of the consolation to be derived by survivors from the consistent Christian life of their deceased friends.* Whenever I think that I have such a son in heaven, I seem to myself to be highly honored. I feel myself unworthy the honor of being so nearly related to one who, judging from the tenor of his life, enjoys so much of his Saviour's love. I would not part with the consolation which *that life* affords for all the treasures of earth.

O, that his mantle might fall on all our youth!

# PUBLICATIONS OF THE AMERICAN TRACT SOCIETY

D'Aubigné's History of the Reformation, a new translation, revised by the Author, 4 vols., ea. 450 pp., cloth extra, $1 75.
Bunyan's Pilgrim's Progress, large type.
Baxter's Saints' Rest, large type.
Life of Jas. Milnor, D.D.
Flavel's Fountain of Life
Flavel's Method of Grace
Flavel's Knocking at the Door.
Mason's Spirit. Treasury
Hall's Scripture History.
Gregory's Letters on Infidelity.
Hopkins on Ten Commandments.
Memoir of Mrs. Graham.
Venn's Complete Duty of Man.
Owen on Forgiveness of Sin, Psalm 130.
Memoir of Mrs. Sarah L. H. Smith.
Sacred Songs, (Hymns and Tunes.)
Ditto, (Patent Notes.)
Paley's Nat'ral Theology
Nelson on Infidelity.
Dr. Spring's Bible not of Man.
Afflicted Man's Companion, by Willison.
Elegant Narratives, select Tracts illustrated.
Memoir of Dr. Payson.
Memoir of Mrs H. L. Winslow.
Memoir of J. B. Taylor.
Memoir of Rev. Dr. Buchanan.
Guide to Y'ng Disciples.
Bunyan's Pilgrim's Prog.
Elijah the Tishbite.
Volume on Infidelity.
Doddridge's Rise and Progress.
Life of Martyn.
Baxter's Saints' Rest.
Edwards' History of Redemption.
Pike's Persuasives to Early Piety.
Practical Piety, by Hannah More.
Anecdotes for the Family Circle.
Spirit of Popery.
Wilberforce's Prac. View
Life of David Brainerd.
Melvill's Bib. Thoughts.
Mammon, or Covetousness the Sin of the Church. By Harris.
Life of Samuel Pearce.
Edwards on Affections.
Mem. of Hannah Hobbie
Life of John Newton.
Gurney on Love to God.
Memoir of H. Page.
Nevins' Pract. Thoughts.
Abbott's Moth. at Home.
Abbott's Child at Home.
Youth's Book of Natural Theology.
Nevins' Thoughts on Popery.
Religion and Eter. Life.
Dibble's Thoughts on Missions.
Morison's Counsels to Young Men.
James' Anxious Inquirer.
Mason's Self-Knowledge
Sherman's Guide to Acquaintance with God.
Divine Law of Beneficence.
Zaccheus, or Scriptural Plan of Benevolence.
James' Young Man from Home.
Child's Book on Repentance.
Henry on Meekness.
Baxter's Call to the Unconverted.
Do., Dying Thoughts
Do., Life, chiefly by himself.
Alleine's Alarm.
Keith's Evidences of Prophecy.
Life of Rev. Samuel Kilpin.
Fuller's Backslider.
Flavel on Keeping the Heart.
Flavel's Touchstone.
Redeemer's Last Command.
Mem. of Chas. H. Porter.
Memoir of Mad. Rumpff and Duch. de Broglie.
Self-Deception.
The Bible True.
Scudder's Appeal to Mothers.
Social Hymns, (large 32mo.)
Hymns to Sacred Songs, (large 32mo.)

## BOOKS FOR THE YOUNG.

Peep of Day.
Line upon Line.
Precept upon Precept.
Memoir of Anzonetta R. Peters.
The Night of Toil.
Legh Richmond's Letters and Counsels.
Advice to a Young Christian.
Memoir of Clementine Cuvier.
Missionary's Daughter.
Tales about the Heathen.
The Dairyman's Daughter, etc.
The Withered Branch Revived.
Scripture Lessons.
Pictorial Tract Primer.
Great Truths.
Grace Harriet.
Rolls Plumbe.
Child'n Invited to Christ
Narratives of Pious Children.
Letters to Little Children, (13 cuts.)
With numerous similar works.

Also, upwards of 1,000 Tracts and Children's Tracts, separate, bound, or *in packets*, adapted for convenient sale by merchants and traders, many of them with beautiful engravings—in English, German, French, Spanish, Portuguese, Italian, Dutch, Danish, Swedish, and Welsh.

www.ingramcontent.com/pod-product-compliance
Lightning Source LLC
LaVergne TN
LVHW050524100826
845148LV00002B/426

*9781425520250*